# ever more
## accurate
## atrocities
## of
## competence

## new &
## selected poems

Also by Jack Shiner

Whispering Sands and Other Poems
Raking Leaves – Poems
Stunning Jagged Edges of Precise Malfunction

# ever more accurate atrocities of competence

## new & selected poems

# Jack Shiner

Whispering Sands Publishing
VACAVILLE, CALIFORNIA
2024

EVER MORE ACCURATE ATROCITIES OF COMPETENCE
NEW AND SELECTED POEMS

**www.jackshiner.com**

This Whispering Sands Publishing softcover edition
first published 2024

First Edition

LCCN 2024903530
LC record available at *https://lccn.loc.gov/*
D2Dv4
ISBN 978-0-922224-18-0 (Special Signed Edition)
ISBN 978-0-922224-15-9 (hardcover)
ISBN 978-0-92224-17-3 (softcover)
ISBN 978-0-922224-16-6 (ebook)

To my wife Jan
Lover and Perfect Equal

# A NOTE ABOUT THIS BOOK

Jack Shiner is retired from the work world, where that journey began as a Newspaper Boy for the Detroit News in the suburbs of Detroit, Michigan where he was born and raised in Royal Oak. And the journey was concluded after a twenty-two year stint as a Stationary Engineer in the San Francisco Bay Area. In between, he worked five teenage summers in a bakery followed by a variety of jobs which included factory work, printing, banking and as a Fire Alarm Systems Inspector and Technician.

The first creative work he recalls inventing was a little song he made up at the age of five as he walked along holding his mother's hand on the streets of Beacon, New York, where the family was living at the time. It was a song he called "The Man with a Big Fat Nose" which, Shiner says, is better left unheard.

Although he created a few little ditties and scribbled down a few lines in his childhood, it wasn't until he was fourteen years old that he felt he was a poet and would continue to be so for life. A poet whose every word should be chiseled into marble and marveled at for all ages to come... (or so the fourteen-year-old Shiner thought at the time).

It was nearly twenty years later when a friend suggested that Shiner should publish a book of his poetry for all the world to see. So, at a time before the Internet and digital printing, Shiner began the work of typing and manually creating layout boards in a garage for each page of a book to be called "Whispering Sands and Other Poems". And it was then, in 1989, when he discovered that selling poetry was about as easy as making a sculpture from air.

Wanting to publish again, but in no hurry to lose money once more, Shiner waited until 2004 to publish his second book "Raking Leaves-Poems". He was amazed to find that printing technology had changed to the point of the whole publishing process being digital. No lay-out boards, not a piece of paper needed to be touched.

A year later, sitting at the dinner table, Shiner's then ten-year-old son Frank asked if he was going to publish a third book. Shiner said, "Yes". Frank asked what it would be called. Shiner said, "Stunning Jagged Edges of Precise Malfunction". Frank went into giggle-fits and Shiner saw that as a positive sign that the right title had been found. And so it was in 2005.

Since then, Shiner has continued to write and presents in this book many new poems, as well as selected poems from his three previous books. And why would he do that? Shiner says:

*I write it*
  *because I've always known*
    *that even if you don't need it...*
      *I do*


NOTE: Please read poetry responsibly.

# Contents

## new Poems

| | |
|---|---|
| POETRY IS A QUIET MUSIC | 1 |
| FIFTY YEARS AGO | 3 |
| IN A DREAM LAST NIGHT | 8 |
| INSIDE US ALL | 10 |
| APPROACHING SIXTY | 11 |
| DELICATELY | 15 |
| THAT ONE SENTENCE | 16 |
| THE UNQUENCHABLE THIRST | 25 |
| VINTAGE | 27 |
| A KICK IN THE PANTS | 29 |
| MUSIC VIDEOS | 38 |
| BEAVER ISLAND | 39 |
| BY MYSELF, ALL ALONE | 40 |
| SCATTERED TO THE WIND | 45 |
| OH, BOY! | 46 |
| BEFORE YOUR TIME | 50 |
| A HELLUVA RIDE | 52 |
| TEN MINUTES FROM NOW | 56 |
| COUSINS | 57 |
| THE MAGAZINE CHALLENGE | 60 |
| TALKING OVER BREAKFAST | 65 |
| YOU JUST NEVER KNOW | 66 |
| I TRULY DO | 73 |
| GRASS FIRES | 75 |
| MAYBE IT'S JUST ME | 77 |
| RAGGED LITTLE SQUARES | 81 |
| NEVER GIVE UP | 84 |
| POETIC ADVICE | 85 |
| WHERE DO I BEGIN? | 86 |
| TINY | 93 |
| TOTALITY | 94 |
| THE RED PADDLE | 98 |
| NO, MAYBE NOT | 105 |
| DEATH DOESN'T HEAL | 106 |
| WITH NO REGRETS | 115 |

ON READING AND WRITING    118
THESE ARE DIFFERENT TIMES    126
THE BEST THING    128
A WEDDING POEM    129
DEATH AND TAXES    130
LIFE ON MIDNIGHT SHIFT    131
GOOD TIMES – GREAT ADVENTURE    132
DON'T QUIT YOUR DAY JOB    136
WE HAVE THE POWER    137
PULLING MY LEG    141
OVER AT RAY'S    145
IF NOT NOW, WHEN?    151
NOW IS ALWAYS NEW    154

## SELECTED POEMS

**FROM
STUNNING JAGGED EDGES
OF PRECISE MALFUNCTION
(2005)**

CROSSROADS    157
A SLOW DRIP    158
THE KISS    160
ONE POINT EIGHT    162
KNOTS    164
JULIUS    166
EMBRACING SHADOWS    171
MY FRONT PAGE    172
EVER-CHANGING    175
ALL IS ONE    176
SAME OLD BLUES    183
THE BLACK SHEEP    184
TIME IS THE TEACHER    185
TWO NEW QUESTIONS    186

# SELECTED POEMS

## FROM
## RAKING LEAVES – POEMS
## (2004)

| | |
|---|---|
| YESTERDAY'S NEWS | 189 |
| INSPIRATION POINT | 191 |
| WANDERING | 192 |
| STURDY POEMS | 196 |
| CORPORATE TEAM PLAYERS | 197 |
| TO TRULY CREATE | 197 |
| AND SOME PEOPLE | 197 |
| THEATRE THOUGHTS | 198 |
| BUSTER'S NEWSSTAND | 200 |
| POETRY IS FOR SISSIES | 203 |
| SAN FRANCISCO MORNING IN L.A. | 204 |
| DEEPER | 206 |
| WINTER MEADOW | 210 |

# SELECTED POEMS

## FROM
## WHISPERING SANDS AND OTHER POEMS
## (1989)

| | |
|---|---|
| SHANGHAIED | 213 |
| SITTING ON THE FRONT PORCH SWING | 216 |
| THE OLD RED BOMBER | 219 |
| WHISPERING SANDS | 222 |
| DRAGON SMOKE | 224 |
| SMALL CHANGE ON THE DRESSER | 228 |
| LIFE | 231 |
| DREAMS | 231 |
| SOME PEOPLE | 231 |
| AS YOU TURN THE PAGE | 232 |

# abstract esoterica

## New Experimental Poems

Diagnostic Twang               235
In Perpetuity                  237
Irresistible Thumbs            239
Heartwarming Belly Wiggles     241
Dangerous Cobblestones         243
Spinning Complexities          245
Illegal Receptacles            247
Muddy Achievement              249

# ever more
## accurate
## atrocities
## of
## competence

## new poems

# POETRY IS A QUIET MUSIC

Poetry is a quiet music
of subtle rhythm and pauses
thoughts and descriptions
expressions-impressions-emotions

Poetry is a quiet music
and it appears that very few hear it
unless someone is singing it in a song

They consume it several times a day
(if someone is singing it in a song)
but if asked if they like poetry
I think most people
(at least, here in America)
would look at you puzzled
(after a pause)
or they may look at you
as if they had just had a sip of sour milk
or a quick whiff of a foul odor

>        *Poetry?!!*
>        *What?*
>        *Really?*

As if it should only be read
by intellectuals or the lonely
or by little old ladies in quaint villages
on Wednesday afternoons
down at the county library
with tea and muffins Mary made

Poetry is a quiet music—
Poetry is an ocean of thought
in a drop of water
But maybe think of it as short stories
or
dare I say
the texting of the literary world?
         (U  R  2 deep... LOL)

I see you smirking—
those of you who are reading this—
because you all know
that I am likely
only preaching to the choir

But maybe—
just maybe—
one person will read this
that has never taken the time
to read a poem before
(unless forced to do so in high school)
and maybe—
just maybe they'll hear it in their mind
and enjoy a poem
(maybe not this one but—)
maybe one that makes them wonder
or one that makes them look away and smile
close the book on their finger to keep their place
and then open it back up and continue to read

Poetry—
     is a pleasing pause
          for a reflective moment

Poetry—
     is an ocean of thought
          in a drop of water

Poetry—

          is a quiet music

# FIFTY YEARS AGO

Breezing up—
A fresh wind from the north
White capped waves
roaring and rushing to the shore
The blues and greens of the water
stretching out to the horizon
The whites and grays of billowing clouds
and gulls gliding over the beach
The classic look and feel
of a Lake Michigan summer day

The deep blue shadows of the clouds
move over the shimmering surface
ever-changing
evermoving
silently southward
swiftly southward

Fifty years ago
I first walked into this log cabin
as an almost-nine-year-old boy
It was unfinished at that point
No water
no power
no front or back porch
no railing on the loft
or on the stairs up to it

It was the first week of July 1965
The first day of July— maybe
I just remember pulling up to it
in a 1964 silver Pontiac Safari station wagon
and Mom saying: *They had promised
it would be done by the first of July
and the kids and I are moving in
and they can just work around us!*

That was that!
(and that's how it was)

We got our drinking water from a hand pump
up the road, behind the Mines family cabin
about a quarter mile north in the woods
and we got our toilet flushing water
by the pailful from the lake itself
Lanterns were the lights at night
and when weather and winds permitted
meals were cooked outside on a campfire

One of the first pieces of business, as I recall
was to get a big propane tank out there

A secondhand gas stove
and an old Norge gas refrigerator
were purchased from the Cromptons in town
who ran a secondhand store on Waukazoo Street
called *Treasures and Trash*
Some of the furnishings
and dishes and pots and pans
came from *Treasures and Trash,* as well

That's the way it was
with the other five cabins
along the shore that summer
(and other cabins that followed)
Secondhand—
used—
Quaint and cozy were the interiors
of all the cabins
and some never changed
Some always kept their hand pumps
and never had running water
or power in their cabins
Only propane
or maybe a little fuel oil stove

Some up here never built cabins
and just set up camp each summer
for the two or three weeks they were here

It was the middle of the Sixties

1965— Smack dab in the middle
and a Middle-Class workingman
could afford a cabin on a lake
with hand-me-down appliances
and the kids could have a summer Up North
in a cabin on a lake with Mom
while Dad worked away the weekdays
and pulled in the driveway to the cabin
after his Friday night drive north

It was 1965
and Beatlemania was sweeping the nation
(Among the young, at least)
The music-filled British Invasion was underway
as Civil Rights and the Viet Nam War
filled the news programs

But up here—
in the evenings that first summer
it was Mom—
reading the local newspaper to us boys
after a day of swimming and hiking
running through the dunes
climbing trees
finding new secret places
or exploring the abandoned house and barn
a mile up the gravel road
and out on the two-lane blacktop that led to town

It was her reading from the newspapers
she bought on go-to-town Saturdays
or us boys reading comic books
and playing board games in the evenings
and on rainy days

Once the power got put in
a radio was added to the entertainment
that could capture the only two or three stations
that could be captured out there
No television
Mom made that off limits

forbidden—
at least for the first few summers
after which a small black and white portable
invaded the cabin
that could pull in two stations with snowy reception
and sometimes one from across the big lake
in another state
another time zone

And back in those days—
this place seemed to be in another time zone
A time zone all its own—
when we may be the only souls on this bay
nine miles from the nearest town
for weeks at a time
and sometimes seeing no one
until Dad pulled in the driveway
around 11 o'clock on Friday nights
and—
all these stories have been told before—

I'm just reaching back fifty years
as a hammer bangs away
at the new place next door
My daily morning dip in the lake done
and it was a quick one
The winds that blew in from the north
all day yesterday
brought the chilly water of the north, as well
but the skies the last two nights
were just perfect for stargazing
No moon
No clouds

My son Frank and I lying on our backs
out in the dunes on the edge of the forest
with billions of stars up above us
and the streaking meteors of the Perseid showers
silently aglow
swiftly moving
fading out

We were out there in the dunes
until three-thirty in the morning
lying on beach towels under the stars
A mound of sand formed under one end
to serve as a pillow

Looking straight into the Universe
The Big Dipper— low and to the left
The Milky Way straight above
and stretching from horizon to horizon

layer upon layer

   beyond the beyond

      and where it all stops—

         ...nobody knows

## IN A DREAM LAST NIGHT

In a dream last night
I was standing in front
of an automatic teller machine
somewhere unrecognizable
generic
and I was transferring money
to all the babysitters
my brothers and I had
during our rambunctious childhood

Maybe my mother paid very well
or maybe the girls were desperate for money
or maybe my mother just begged
or used the babysitter's mother
to influence the arrangement

However it happened
we ended up with a babysitter
But not always the same one
and I think we went through
every teenage girl in the neighborhood

A wag of the finger from Mom
as she and Dad walked out the door
for an evening of square dancing
telling us boys to be good
while wishing for the miracle
that it may actually happen—
once—
just once

There was Beverly
who would rap us on the knees
with a wooden spoon
usually for quickly blurting out a naughty word
and then pretending none of us said it
while we all sat there
looking at each other giggling—
    *Tit*

There was Kathy
who would give up
and put us to bed way too early
But once that happened
we learned to leave the gate open
and up against the house
under our bedroom window
so we could open the window
crawl out
run to the front door
knock
and run away

And there was Mrs. Culver
who may have been the last resort
when all the teenage girls
had excuses about studying for exams
or dances they had to go to
But Mrs. Culver had no unusual punishments
I think she kept us in line pretty well
But I do recall her
cornering me on the front porch
and forcing me to eat *green peas*

I didn't ask for that spoonful
of nasty, wrinkled green peas
but she was damn sure
that little brat Jacky
was going to eat his green peas
at least until she got that spoon in my mouth
and my gag reflex started

All the babysitters' names came onto the screen
of the ATM in my dream
as one by one
I transferred five thousand dollars to each

Well deserved!

But somehow, I feel—
I'm still getting the better end of the deal

# INSIDE US ALL

Inside us all
dwells a feeling of anger
of the way things generally are—
War
The cost of living
The corrupt regularity of politics
Injustice

Inside us all
is a hidden sense of hopelessness
that nothing will change—
Oh, well—
We will shrug our shoulders
turn away
and accept it all as the way it is

Inside us all
Is the power to change—
A sense of right and wrong
A sense that good deeds can be done
A sense that peace can prevail
That the world can be well—
   fair—
      just

Inside us all
we know that what is evil
corrupt
unfair
unjust
is only a shadow
A shadow that can fade
dissolve and disappear
when bathed in light

And the light is there—
   shining brightly
      warmly—
         inside us all

# APPROACHING SIXTY

I seem to fart more—
Let's get that bit of unpleasant business
out of the way
right up front and center, shall we?
Done with—
OK?
And maybe that's where the term
"Old Fart" came from
I don't know
There may be some truth to that

But there is some truth to this:
I can tell you
that while I'm approaching sixty
I'm not as flexible as I used to be—
I mean joints and muscles
especially the hips
The aches and pains seem to increase

I don't want this to sound
like a bunch of whining and complaining
I'm just laying out some observations

I'm not saying
that you start dwelling on the end
(at least I don't)
but you do start thinking about the next phase:
The Retirement Years
You start the countdown

It used to be a long way off—
So distant that you didn't recognize
what that little speck out on the horizon was

But then—
the next thing you know
you're within a ten-year window
and you think to yourself:
That was a long, long road

So—
how did I get here so quickly?

No—
I wouldn't say I'm dwelling on the end
but the death of a parent
and all the aunts and uncles
as they leave one by one—
and with the passing of each one
you *are* one step closer
to *being*— The Older Generation

That phase is somewhat expected—
(the parents and aunts and uncles)
but when friends your own age
or just a few years older start passing
it brings a tightness to your throat
a tear to your eye
a pause of silence—
and reflective thinking

Damn!
They never got to retire
They never got to know any leisure
(beyond a two- or three-week vacation)
they never got to see the places
they wanted to see
or do the things
they wanted to do
or see the grandkids grow

And that's why I want to tell you—
about this drum set

You see—
as I was approaching sixty
I had guitars
I had a banjo
but I never had a drum set
with bronze cymbals
and chrome hardware—

BOOM BOOM BANG BANG
RAT-A-TAT-TAT
PSSSSSSsssssshhhhhhhhhhhhhhhh—

And as I'm approaching sixty
there are certain decisions I make
after I deliberate
and weigh things out
and I end up with the answer being:
Why not?

Yeah—
Why not?
A drum set?
Why not?

So, on a whim—
I look around—
and I find a drum set that's two years old
and as the story goes:
The parents bought their son this drum set
two years ago when he was sixteen
and the guys he was in a band with
were two years older than he was
So, they hit eighteen
and off to college they go
and *Pfffft!* goes the band
and now he's eighteen
and off to college goes the kid
and the parents say
    *Please, we just want more space*
    *You can have it all for $400 cash*
Wow!
Really?
This is like, $900 worth of drum set here
So, yeah—
Why not?

So, look—
All I'm saying is
do what you need to do

Go where you need to go
See what you need to see

I'm not telling you all
to go out and buy a drum set
I'm not saying it's a cure for anything
or that it holds any magical powers
And sometimes I sit behind it
and say to myself
    *Are you nuts?*
But I'm having fun
I'm doing something
I've always wanted to do
I'm learning something
I've always wanted to learn

And if you're waiting to get to heaven
and think it's all going to happen there—
do your thing—
I'm not here to tell you you're wrong
But I can tell you
that in the here and now
there are parents out there saying
    *Please, we just want the space*
    *Put this in the back of your truck and go*
    *Have fun— knock yourself out*

And as I'm approaching sixty—
Yeah, maybe I fart more—
but as long as you keep your distance
and I fart in time with the music
maybe no one will notice

## DELICATELY

I long for times to be less tense
to travel
to wander along our way
Each day, a new adventure

To pause—
  if we wish

For hours—
  if need be—
just to ponder the light and shadows
as they move and meander
and melt into a sunset's glow

Feel the breeze—
  delicious

Listen as the evening fades
  and the night descends—

    delicately

# THAT ONE SENTENCE

This subject
seems to trigger the tempers of some people

It is a subject that can be vague
confusing
distorted and heated—
all at the same time

And by writing about it
I'm not intending to stir anything up
or ignite anyone's temper
I just intend to examine it
and you may examine it with me—
if you wish

This examination
begins with something seen to be vague
and it was written like this:

> *A well-regulated militia, being necessary
> to the security of a free state, the right of
> the people to keep and bear arms, shall not
> be infringed.*

Yes
that is the second amendment
of the Constitution of the United States

And it is an amendment
that is not pages long
or of several paragraphs—
It is one sentence long
Twenty-seven words from beginning to end
with three commas and one period

Arguments have arisen
especially over the past few decades
concerning what that one sentence means

Some people and organizations
will completely ignore the first thirteen words
and simply read the last fourteen as:
>    *...the right of the people to keep and bear arms,*
>    *shall not be infringed.*

One gun rights organization
has only those last fourteen words
emblazoned upon the walls
of the main lobby entrance
of their world headquarters

But there is only one period in that one sentence
So, should the first thirteen words
be ignored and separated from the rest
and therefore, intentionally omitted?

And, if taken as a whole sentence
don't most sentences in the English language
begin with the principal subject
being referred to?

>    *The big brown dog, curling up in front of*
>    *the warm fireplace, sighed deeply, yawned*
>    *and closed its eyes to sleep*

Is the principal subject of that sentence
the warm fireplace?
Sighing and yawning?
Sleep?
Or the big brown dog?
I would think the big brown dog
is the principal subject of that one sentence

So—
is "*A well-regulated militia*"
the principal subject of that one sentence
that is the second amendment?

At the time
when it was being debated

in the summer of 1787
as to whether we needed
the Constitution of the United States
there was already a document in place
called the Articles of Confederacy
    and Perpetual Union

Also, at this time
people were writing essays
and distributing pamphlets
arguing the pros and cons
of replacing the Articles of Confederacy
with a new Constitution

The most famous of these essays
that have been passed down to us through time
became collectively known as
    The Federalist Papers
which were essays distributed at the time
as being written by *Publius*
An anonymous source

Why anonymous?
I think it was due to the fact
that there was not yet a Bill of Rights
and therefore
there was not yet freedom of speech
or freedom of the press

And so, these names for authors were used
such as *Publius*
to remain anonymous
For example
one that Benjamin Franklin used was
    *Silence Dogood*

*Publius*
eventually became known to us
as Alexander Hamilton
James Madison
and to a lesser extent John Jay

In The Federalist Papers
Alexander Hamilton describes
a well-regulated militia this way:

*"To oblige the great body of yeomanry, and of other class-
es of the citizens, to be under arms for the purpose of going
through military exercises and evolutions, as often as might
be necessary to acquire the degree of perfection which would
entitle them to the character of a well-regulated militia..."*

He then ends this paragraph with:

*"Little more can reasonably be aimed at, with respect to the peo-
ple at large, then to have them properly armed and equipped;
and in order to see that this be not neglected, it will be neces-
sary to assemble them once or twice in the course of a year."*

Which sounds like our current National Guard
whose origins date back to 1636

Between those two parts of the paragraph
he argues that to obtain that "degree of perfection"
the country may lose too much
in the way of productivity
by taking men away from their farms and shops

So, let them be properly armed and equipped
and assemble them once or twice a year
to go through military exercises

OK—
So, then in the document in place at the time
called the Articles of Confederacy
which preceded the Constitution
you will find this written
in Article VI, Section IV:

*...every State shall always keep up a regular and well-disci-
plined militia, sufficiently armed and accoutered, and shall
provide and constantly have ready for use, in public stores,*

a due number of field pieces and tents, and a proper quantity
of arms, ammunition, and camp equipage."

So, it would seem it was the State
who was to supply the arms and ammunition
to maintain a regular
and well-disciplined militia

OK— Let's try to break this down:
Alexander Hamilton at the time
describes a well-regulated militia
as being under arms to acquire a degree of perfection
through military exercises
The Articles of Confederacy stated
that it was the State
who was to supply the arms
ammunition and equipage

Then we have the second amendment
which states:
> A well-regulated militia, being necessary
> to the security of a free state, the right of
> the people to keep and bear arms, shall not
> be infringed.

And also, there was the Senate edited version
of the original proposal
of then-Congressman James Madison
who introduced the following to the floor:

> "The right of the people to keep and bear arms shall not be
> infringed; a well-armed, and well-regulated militia being
> the best security of a free country; but no person religious-
> ly scrupulous of bearing arms, shall be compelled to render
> military service in person."

This was put to the floor by Madison
as a remedy to the protests of five of the states
who did not want the proposed Federal Government
to have a standing army
preferring State militias instead

And although his sentence starts with:
    *"The right of the people to keep and bear arms"*
everything he mentions
has to do with militias and national security
and even included a reference
to it being an all-volunteer military
which the Senate struck
from the final draft

It would make perfect sense in colonial America
and this newly formed United States
to allow citizens to keep and bear arms
so that when the cannon was fired
or the church bell rang
(or whatever the prearranged signal was
for the militia to assemble)
that they would all report
to the location of assembly already armed
without having to first go to the public stores building
where the State stored the equipment

To be in a state of readiness
this makes sense:
The State would provide the arms
and the citizens of the well-regulated militia
would keep and bear those arms

Now—
Here's an observation
that may trigger a few tempers

And this is a key
and arguably sensitive point of observation
which is to say
that the second amendment states
    *to keep and bear arms*
but it does not state
    *to purchase and own arms*
only to keep and bear arms
Were those arms
to be provided by the State

for the purpose
of having a well-regulated militia?
You be the judge

So—
there's the observation
and here comes my opinion:
In terms of gun ownership
I have no problem with arms being owned
as I saw them owned when I was a kid
growing up in the Sixties
that is to say
Dads in the neighborhood had hunting rifles
and although I wasn't aware of it at the time
I suppose some of the neighbors
may have had a pistol or shotgun in the house
for protection of the home
and I understand that—
That's reasonable and responsible
But is it reasonable and responsible
to "open carry" a loaded firearm in public?
In a hardware store?
Coffee shop?
Park or parade?

At the time of the adoption of the Constitution
I think it was a given fact
that as a means of survival
everyone had hunting arms
and arms to protect loved ones and property
from raids or thieves
That is reasonable and responsible

It may have been such a point of reality
given fact and common sense
that it never crossed the minds
of our Founding Fathers
to even mention it in the Constitution
And given the writings of that time
by our Founding Fathers
as well as sentence structure of the English language

I think the second amendment—
that one sentence—
is concerned with a Well-Regulated Militia
and not individual gun ownership

Now—
if you go back and look at the statistics of the Sixties
when Dads owned hunting rifles
and people had a pistol or a shotgun in the house
for home protection
how many school shootings were there?
How many mass shootings in theatres?
In town squares, grocery stores or churches?

How many mass shootings are there now
in Canada?
Australia?
New Zealand?
In Europe?
In Japan?

And you would think that the mass murder
of twenty schoolchildren
five and six-year-olds
(and six adult staff members)
while peacefully sitting in their classrooms
learning their ABCs
would be enough to trigger Congress
The White House
and the Supreme Court to take action
to do something
anything
You would think so

But instead
they proved to us citizens
definitively and undeniably
what useless cowards most of them really are

Five and six-year-olds
murdered in their classrooms

with such a powerful weapon
that some parents had to give DNA samples
for mangled remains to be identified as their child
while these useless cowards in Congress do nothing
and apparently feel no shame
in being useless cowards and doing nothing

And here's a thought for those who feel
that unlimited gun ownership is the in the spirit
of what the Founding Fathers intended in 1791
when the Bill of Rights was ratified:
How about in keeping with the spirit of 1791
that unlimited gun ownership applies only to firearms
that were developed and in production in 1791?

Wouldn't that be closer
to what the Founding Fathers may have been thinking?

I didn't mean to start ranting—
but there it is—
a simple observation—
which was triggered by reading the Constitution
the Articles of Confederacy
the Federalist Papers
the Bill of Rights
and that one sentence

Peace

# THE UNQUENCHABLE THIRST

So—
my son looks up from his plate this evening
while sitting at the dinner table
looks at me and says:

*What would it feel like to be inside-out?*

Ummm—
Well—
It's not something that has crossed my mind
recently... if ever
In fact
I rather like not being inside out
Thank you very much

*Well then...*
*what if the world was spinning so fast*
*that we would levitate above the ground?*

It would make for some
interesting new dance moves
I guess

*And what if we lived in a place*
*where it was dark six months of the year?*
*I think I would like that*

Well... you wouldn't have to worry
about finding your sunglasses for a long time
I suppose

*And what if we could go to school at night*
*and sleep during the day?*

*Do your eyes have a lot of tiny mirrors inside*
*and that's how we see?*

*How do atoms bombs work*
*and does it have something to do with plasma?*

*Are some plants consumers?*

Ahhhh...
the inquisitive
non-stop imagination of the young mind

The never-ending questions
and the unquenchable thirst for the answers
the knowledge
the truth

And the challenge your own brain faces
when confronted with a question like:

*Why is water wet?*

# VINTAGE

There is a "vintage" guitar market out there
(for those of you who don't know)
and there are actually people who pay $25,000
or even $40,000 or $50,000
for a 50 or 60-year-old
solid body electric guitar

My first reaction is:
C'mon, people—
we're talking about a slab of wood
cut out on a band saw here
For cryin' out loud!
Are you nuts?!

We're not talking about a Stradivarius violin
made in Cremona, Italy in the 17th century
We're talking about a mass-produced slab of wood
cut out on a band saw in a factory somewhere
What are you thinking?

Aside from that—
everything is old
The frets and other parts are worn
Face the facts here:
It's an old used guitar being *called* "vintage"

$25,000?
$40,000?
$50,000?

Here's the way it all breaks down for me:
Maybe for one that's in really good shape
well kept
I'd give you $1,000
It's an old used guitar, after all

So—
for those of you paying $25,000
forgive me for saying so

but what you are really paying
is $1,000 for an old used guitar
and a $24,000 Stupidity Tax

There's a sucker born every minute—
I mean—
take a moment and think about this—
Who do you think is setting those prices?
Guitar store owners and collectors
who are out to fleece someone—
that's who—

Is the "vintage" market
just another modern-day version
of "The Emperor's New Clothes"?

There's a sucker born every minute—
and perhaps I'll pay that Stupidity Tax too someday
(if I'm lucky enough to be in the position to do so)
  but—
    then again—
      probably not

# A KICK IN THE PANTS

Of the many misunderstandings
I have heard about Unions
are these three:
> You can't fire bad performers
> They all get paid too much and
> They get raises they don't deserve

In my thirty-one years in Unions
as a worker
and as an Assistant Chief Engineer
I've known bad performers
and I've seen them fired
(Or leave if they felt challenged or unwelcome
because they were getting disciplined)

The bottom line is this:
If you have bad performers
who are not being coached or disciplined
it's because you have a weak Chief
who is allowing bad performance
to exist on their crew

A myth prevails
among the general public
that once hired
a Union employee
can do whatever they want to do
without consequence

That they can sit down
put their feet up on the table
twiddle their thumbs all day
and not a thing can be done about it
Not true
The same processes are in place
as they are at any corporation:
> Verbal warnings
> Written evaluations and coaching
> Written discipline and suspensions

Written exit interviews
and termination

If there are weak performers
who continue to be weak performers
there is weak management of the crew—
Period

Yes, they can be fired
I have seen it done
and in some cases
it went straight to the last step:
Termination
Immediately

For two reasons I have seen this done
and with the support of the Union
        1) Theft
        2) Physical violence or threat thereof
Here's what you did
Hand over your keys and company ID badge
There's the door
Goodbye and good luck

Terminations for other reasons
can be long and tedious
because some weak performers just never learn
or think they'll never be terminated
Tardiness
Absenteeism
Insubordination
Lack of performance
Falsification of daily work logs
It all takes time
But I have seen people terminated
for any of the above reasons

Can a Union employee be fired?
Absolutely
I've seen it done
and in each case I've seen

the termination was justified

I've been in Union meetings at the Union Hall
where this topic was discussed
where I have heard Union officers say:
>*Guys*
>*when you clock in*
>*give your employers*
>*an honest day's work*
>*and if you get terminated*
>*for poor performance or not showing up*
>*or you're caught on camera stealing*
>*or sleeping on the job*
>*What do you want us to do about it?*
>*How can we defend it?*
>*Why would we defend it?*
>*Just do the job you're getting paid to do*

And if you think a Union employee
is getting paid too much
it's probably because
you're not getting paid enough

When it comes to asking for a raise—
for you, it may just be one-on-one
You ask
They say not this year
You walk away dismayed
angered
perhaps planning your exit

If you don't have
Collective Bargaining behind you
it's only you—
all alone

But—
if the entire crew says:
>*We want a cost-of-living raise*
>*or we all walk out in ten days*
Then you get their attention

And keep this in mind—
A Union contract is called
a Collective Bargaining Agreement

It's an agreement between the Employer
and the Employees
and if the conditions weren't agreed to
the agreement would not have been signed

If you don't have a fair wage
If you don't have a pension
If you don't have adequate health care
If you don't have safe working conditions
then you don't have Collective Bargaining behind you

And from my thirty-one years in the Union
I never once got a raise
of more than 3%
not once

Some years 1%
Some 2%
Most 3%
but never more than 3%
and that's a cost-of-living raise

My rent went up more than 3% per year
Gas, food, utilities, taxes
Even at 3% per year you can't keep up with it

And one year
it went right to the eleventh hour
of the contract negotiations
Literally

We were asking for 3%
and another 5 cents per hour towards our pensions
The corporation said No—

Picket signs were taken from trunks of cars
handed out and taken home

and then about ten minutes to midnight
we were all contacted
to go to work as scheduled
A temporary agreement had been reached

And I'd like you to understand this:
That year we were only asking for 3%
and that same year
the CEO of this corporation
who was already receiving
7.7 million dollars a year
was given a 2.2 million dollar raise
to 9.9 million dollars a year
but they didn't want us
to have a 3% cost-of-living raise
and another 5 cents per hour given to our pension
and without Collective Bargaining
we would not have gotten that

Does everyone deserve that 3% raise?
No
but if they hadn't been warned
or coached or disciplined or terminated
that's the fault of a weak
and ineffective Chief of the crew
not the Union

And if you think the Merit System
is the only way to give raises—
 *Pssst— C'mere—*
 *Have I gotta a story for you!*

Before I was in Unions for thirty-one years
I worked as a non-Union bank employee
So, I know about the one-on-ones
where you ask for a raise and are denied
But—
I know something more

I know that I was once non-Union
and had the same misunderstandings

that the general public has
and that in my first book of poetry
published in 1989
there is a poem I wrote berating Unions
The Musician's Union in particular
because I thought the San Francisco Symphony
was on strike for more money
but I found out later that the strike
was actually about health care issues
My bad— for not doing better research

But I know something more—
I know the dark side of merit raises

At one point
I was a bank officer
in charge of fourteen employees
at the main office of a bank downtown
in the Financial District of San Francisco
A young twenty-something salaried
overworked bank officer
in a three-piece suit
necktie
briefcase
pocket watch in one vest pocket
a watch chain looping over to the other pocket
cowboy boots on my feet
Yeah—picture that

Salary
Not paid by the hour
Big mistake
because I was working
an average of sixty hours a week
sometimes more
No overtime pay
and when I'd have a one-on-one
asking for a raise from a Manager
I would hear this:
> Jack, you're not paid by the hour
> you're paid for results

*and, frankly, I just don't see the results*
and when asked why I thought
I needed a raise I'd hear:
>*Jack, I asked for reasons*
>*and, frankly, all I hear are excuses*
>*Is there anything else I can help you with?*

Among my duties
I was to write evaluations for the fourteen employees
and they were all due the same month
So, I was working extra hours
and coming in on my days off
to get all this done

The ranking on these went like this:
>1 - Consistently exceeds goals
>2 - Meets and sometimes exceeds goals
>3 - Meets goals
>4 - Needs improvement
>5 - Exit interview and termination

Here's the first dark secret:
We were always told to put in one goal
that could never be achieved

With that one goal in place
the employee could never get a 1
and arguments could be made
that they didn't earn a 2 or a 3
because they did not meet all their goals
and if you haven't caught on by now—
raises were based on how high you ranked

So—
I was told that everyone had to have this goal:
>*One million dollars in new loans*
but here was the problem—
we weren't in the Loan Department
Some were Tellers
Some were behind the scenes
and had no contact with the public

Could any of them bring in
one million dollars in new loans?
No—
but that was the plan
One unachievable goal
so that they ranked lower
and got a lower, if any, raise
but—
it gets worse

I did my fourteen evaluations
and gave everybody a 2
because they all worked hard
and deserved a raise of some sort

I handed them in to the Vice President
and was called into her office the next morning

I sat down
She looked at me with a scowl
tossed the fourteen evaluations
across the desk towards me and said
  *Do them again*
I said Why?
  *Because you gave them all twos*
But that reflects my crew and they deserve raises
  *Yeah, well that's not in the budget*

She then proceeded to tell me what I was to do:
I was to rewrite all the evaluations
One person was to get a 1 and a raise
One person was to get a 4 and a threat
Everybody else gets a 3 and no raise

I looked at her and said
  But that's not a true reflection of my crew
She scowled even deeper
and setting her teeth on edge
she hissed at me:
  *Well, that's the budget*
  *So, just— do it!*

And so, from my experience
the merit-raise system
isn't worth the paper it's written on

Give people a cost-of-living raise
and for performances above and beyond
give them a bonus of some sort
And if the person deserves neither
write them up
show them the door
and give them a little raise—
by giving them a kick in the pants
on their way out

Goodbye
    and good luck

## MUSIC VIDEOS

Music videos
and how best to watch them

Step One:
press START

Step Two:
close your eyes and listen

Step Three:
When the music stops
open your eyes

Step Four:
press STOP

(Unless you really liked the music
in which case you may return
to Step One)

## BEAVER ISLAND

Island life
Quiet
Calm
Winds whispering through the pines
rippling the green-blue surface
stretching out to the horizon
of this beautiful Great Lake

Islands in the distance
Hog
Garden
Squaw
Whiskey
and the mainland of Michigan beyond

There's a great big world out there
but here—
it's just the wind and the waves
whispering
and winding their way
   to somewhere
      deep within

## BY MYSELF, ALL ALONE

I think back
to being seventeen years old
and the many times I left the house
to take a walk in the evening
by myself
all alone
after saying to my Folks
   *I'll be right back*
   *Just going out for a walk*
And sometimes
it was just a walk around the block
to get some air
to just get out and think about things
or sneak a cigarette
as I walked around those suburban Detroit
neighborhood streets

Sometimes I'd walk a block and a half
to 13 Mile Road to a little store
for a candy bar and a soda pop
or a bag of chips and an iced tea

Sometimes I'd go in the other direction
and walk a little farther west
out to Woodward Avenue
along Starr Road
past Memorial Park
where another little store was

In our neighborhood
we called these "party stores"
In most places they seem to be called
"Mom and Pops"

On this corner
there was also a "Coney Island" diner
where you could get a hot dog with chili on it
and some yellow mustard
if you please

But mostly I just went there
to sit at the counter and have a coffee
It was only ten cents back then
and I could usually come up with that
and sit and talk with the guy behind the counter

Generally, only one guy worked there
at any given time in the evening
and with it being pretty slow
they were probably happy
to have someone to talk to
One of the guys was Gino

I'd put a dime on the counter
Gino would pour a cup and we would talk
I don't remember about what
maybe girls
maybe music
maybe the cars going by on Woodward Avenue

But during all these walks
as a seventeen-year-old
through those suburban Detroit streets
no one ever stopped me
No one bothered me
Nobody saw me with my long hair
and black leather jacket
and asked what I was doing there
or felt threatened by me

I think about those many walks
because there's a seventeen-year-old
who was murdered down in Florida
for doing exactly what I used to do
as a seventeen-year-old:
taking a walk in the evening
by myself
all alone
to a little store
maybe for some candy and an iced tea
as he did the evening he was murdered

His name was Trayvon
and as he was walking back
a man started to follow him
A man with a gun
concealed under his coat

The man wasn't following Trayvon to rob him
or kidnap him
The man claimed to be on "neighborhood watch"
and I guess he didn't like the looks
of this seventeen-year-old
walking by himself
all alone

The man called the police first
to report someone suspicious
and he sounded a bit angry
frustrated—
a bit winded on the recorded call

The person at police dispatch
asked if he was following the person
and the man said *Yeah*
with some words to the effect
of saying that this person was a punk
and was up to something
The police dispatcher said
　　　　*No, we don't want you to follow him*

Apparently, the man with the gun
was a "wanna-be" cop
and the problem with these guys
and some other gun owners
is that having possession of that gun
is the same as a ten-year-old
with a pack of firecrackers:
Just looking at those firecrackers is not enough
Just possessing them is not enough
He needs to find a way
and any reason at all
to light one off

And although the police dispatcher
asked him not to follow the "suspicious" person
he did
and a confrontation happened
that resulted in seventeen-year-old Trayvon
lying on the ground
dying
with a bullet through his heart
A seventeen-year-old
armed only with his cell phone
some candy
and an iced tea

And it took an astounding 44 days—
44 days before the police arrested the murderer
44 days because the murderer said
he did it in self-defense

44 days on his word alone
and I think, in all of this
the most sickening thing he said
was that what happened was "God's Plan"

Think for a moment—
how cowardly and pathetic that statement is
The murder of a seventeen-year-old
walking back from the store was God's Plan

The murderer was put on trail
and found Not Guilty
Acquitted
by a Florida jury of six

I think about those many times
I took walks in the evening at seventeen
by myself
all alone

Are you telling me
that I could have been murdered at seventeen
because someone thought I looked suspicious?

Are you telling me that the murderer
would have been found Not Guilty
by saying it was done in self-defense
on his word alone
and that it was God's Plan?

I asked myself these simple questions:
Would seventeen-year-old Trayvon
still be alive today
if the murderer had stayed in his car?
If he had not followed Trayvon?
If he had not had a gun?
The answer is yes
Trayvon would still be alive

The choices were the murderer's
and he made those choices alone
He had the gun
He got out of his car
He followed Travon
He created the situation
where a murder took place
with a gun that he owned

Are you telling me
that justice was done?

I think the answer is: No

I think the system failed us
in an awful, horribly tragic way
and being of that opinion
I don't think I'm by myself
all alone

Do you?

## SCATTERED TO THE WIND

Scattered to the wind we become
by circumstance
by necessity
on a whim, perhaps

Like a dandelion
that becomes a puff of white
then individual seeds with parachutes
carried away by the winds of change
to land where they will
and do the best they can
with what they have at the moment
A game of chance

Sometimes never intending to put down roots
Sometimes not able to— remaining temporary
until temporary takes on a new meaning
and a few months
becomes a few years
a few decades
and life moves on
while you're busy doing the best you can
with what you have at the moment
and there's nothing wrong with that—
that's life—

And the place where you start
is a place purely picked
by Chance and Circumstance

Do the best you can
with what you've got
so long as it is reasonable
and harms no one—
        including yourself—

Scattered to the wind we become

# OH, BOY!

Oh, Boy—
John is gone
although most people wouldn't know it

He was one of those singer-songwriters
who had been writing
performing and recording songs
just shy of fifty years
and maybe you never knew his name
but you have probably heard
at least one of his songs
as sung by someone other than himself

He was a "Songwriter's Songwriter"
admired by anyone
who ever sat down with pen and paper
and a guitar on their lap
or sat down at a piano, maybe

All those other songwriters
who at one time or another
slapped their forehead
with the palm of their hand
after hearing one of his songs
and said softly to themselves
> *Damn—*
> *Why didn't I think of that?*

His songs were filled with good ideas
common sense
heart and soul
and the honest observations
of an honest man

An honest young Chicago mailman
who like other songwriters thought:
> *Well, I don't have a pretty voice*
> *so, I better make up for that*
> *with my songwriting*

46

and Oh, Boy, did he!

The first time I heard of him
my wife and I were teenagers—
not that we were husband and wife
when we were teenagers—
We were just friends then
But I think the key to a great marriage
is to marry someone
who was first a friend
but that's another subject for another poem
at another time
and don't you go writing a song about it either
That's my idea
Go get your own ideas

Well— anyway—
where was I?

Oh yeah—
we were teenage friends, us two
and one night we were listening to records
at my parents' house in the living room
and she says
> *Ya got any of this guy?*
and I say
> *No, I never heard of that guy*
and she says
> *Well, ya gotta hear this guy*
and I say
> *OK, I'll go find a record by that guy*
and she says
> *It's the one with this guy on front*
> *sitting on a bale of hay*
and I say
> *Hay? OK!*

At least
I think that's the way
the conversation unfolded

We were teenage friends
the two of us
just listening to records
in my parents' living room

And so, I went out and got the record
with that guy on the front
sitting on a bale of hay
and Oh, Boy, did I like it!

The wit and wisdom in the words
The melodies of his fingerpicking
on a six-string acoustic guitar
and over the many, many years since then
the many, many songs of his we've heard

In time, he started his own record company
and he called it
　　　Oh, Boy! Records

And he said he called it Oh, Boy! Records
so that when he had a good year
he could say with excitement
　　　*Oh, Boy! LOOK at those RECORD sales!*
and when he had a bad year
he could say with disappointment
　　　*Oh, Boy! Look at THOSE record sales!*

Oh, Boy!
John is gone
A victim of the Corona Virus

When we heard the news
tears came to my wife's eyes
My tears came the next morning
when I posted some of his lyrics
on a board in the shop I worked at
where I usually posted a Joke-of-the-Day

But that day I posted this:

*"Father forgive us for what we must do*
*You forgive us, we'll forgive you*
*We'll forgive each other 'til we both turn blue*
*then we'll whistle and go fishing in heaven"*
*-John Prine, American songwriter*
*Died of Corona Virus, age 73*
*April 7, 2020*

John is gone...
Oh, Boy...

## BEFORE YOUR TIME

It's that time of year again
to get poked and prodded
and measured and scanned
and x-rayed
and *Open, please*
*Say 'Ah'*
*Let's take a look in here, shall we?*
*How's your diet?*
*Are you exercising?*
*Tell me a little about your family*
*Bend this way*
*Stretch back*
*Touch your toes*
*Drop your drawers*
*Turn your head*
*Cough, Uh-huh*
*Now cough again*
*Very good*
*Bend over and—*

Whoa there!
No guy enjoys that little poke!
Those few uncomfortable seconds

But those few uncomfortable seconds
can save your life, Guys
Can save you from a few years of pain
as you feel your insides
being eaten alive by cancer

Hmmmm... let me think about this choice:
      A) Years of being eaten alive by cancer or
      B) A few uncomfortable seconds
         of an undignified poke

I guess I'll take the poke, please
The undignified poke

Think of it as preventative maintenance, Guys

Think of it as...
looking under the hood and checking the oil
Yeah—
See that all those hose clamps are tight
Kick the tires
Check the fluids
Make sure all the caps are secure
because you just never know

You just never know, Guys
And there's been far too many men
who have died in their early fifties
all because they just refused to undergo
a few uncomfortable seconds of examination—
that undignified poke

(Even though it may have saved their lives)

Get that oil checked, Guys
Kick the tires
Tighten those nuts and bolts
and don't let yourself fall apart
before your time

# A HELLUVA RIDE

Among the wonderful gifts I was given
is one that I am using now:
A coffee cup
And on it is written
> *Retirement Weekly Schedule:*
> *Do Whatever The Hell I Want To Do*

So, here I am
on the morning of Day One
doing whatever the Hell I want to do:
Sipping a black coffee
and writing a poem

I have to say
that a sense of peace
did settle over me yesterday
knowing that I didn't have to face
the possibility of running face first
into a hornet's nest on this Monday
Any Monday morning was like that

This wasn't the kind of business
where you walked out the door Friday
knowing that you will take up
exactly where you left off
when you open the door on Monday

No
It was a twenty-four hour
seven-days-a-week business
of fixing whatever went wrong
and things don't stop going wrong
just because it's your weekend

The position I had
as the Assistant Chief Engineer
was something like
walking into the shop in the morning
and putting a dog collar on

except—
there wasn't just one place on the collar
to attach a leash—
No— there were about a dozen
and the leashes would get tugged on
and yanked from all directions
all day long

Sometimes quickly and sharply
until you walked out the door that evening
thinking that this could be a night
for two fingers of Scotch on-the-rocks

All day long
the leashes are getting tugged on
Yanking you in this direction
Now that direction
and rarely in the direction
that you had planned to go

And in this age of technology
it is not only people
walking up to your office door
or catching sight of you in the hallway
It is the desk phone
cell phone
texting
emails
A two-way radio on your belt
and little windows
that pop up on the monitor screen
asking if you are available
It is just non-stop

And you just have to draw the line somewhere
For me, that was the bathroom door

When I went into the bathroom
the radio and cell phone were not answered
*Let me pee in peace, will ya?*
*For cryin' out loud!*

As the new Assistant Chief Mike put it:
> *Wow—*
> *This is like waking up*
> *on a roller coaster!*

Yeah—
Welcome to the circus
It is exactly like that some days

You are secured into your seat
and *click-clack-click-clack*
the car slowly inches up
the first steep incline
as you smile to yourself and say:
> *Oh, man!*
> *What did I get myself into?*

Too late—
No stopping this now

The car continues to climb
as the chains and cables go
*click-clack-click-clack*
and then— WHOOOOOSH!
Off you go!
> *Clickety-clack*
> *Clickety-clack*
> *Clickety-clickety-clickety-clack*

Whoa!
Rushing down at break-neck speed
down over up and around
this way and that way
> *HANG ON!!!*
> *YEEEE-HAAAAA!!!!*

And in a blur—
it all rushes by so fast
so fast
and it will
Believe me, it will

54

Before you know it
and seemingly without much notice
the car slows to a stop
the bar raises up
and you can rise and walk away

Maybe a little unsteady, at first
Shaking your head with a smile
looking back at it all
and thinking to yourself
>  *Wow—*
>  *That was a helluva ride!*

## TEN MINUTES FROM NOW

I had a little something
that I was going to write down
but I either got distracted
or lazy
one or the other
or both

But the point of writing this down is this:
If I don't remember what it was—
If it wasn't memorable to me—
why would I think
it would be memorable to anyone else?

This is why I also don't record
every little musical idea
that comes into my head

I'll let it go a day or two
then go back and see if the idea is still there
and if it wasn't memorable to me
I wouldn't expect it to be memorable to you

So—
yeah—
ten minutes from now
I'll probably forget about this poem...

        ...you probably will too

# COUSINS

There is a deep tension
between the Black and White races in this country
that never seems to fade away
and, even today, there are people
both Black and White
who feel a deep, blind hatred
for every individual of a race
without ever meeting them—
They just hate the whole race— they just do

To those who harbor this hatred
I'd like to share something with you
Something I have learned
Something that might disturb you
and that something is this:
   You may be cousins

I say this
because of something I have learned
about myself
about the past

In these modern times
I had my DNA tested
and started searching my ancestry
on an Internet site
and part of this ancestry service
is to keep you up to date
with who has been joining
who may share some DNA with you
With categories of cousins:
First cousins, second cousins
and as far out as sixth to eighth cousins

To be a seventh cousin
you would share a sixth Great-Grandfather
and you have 128 of those

In my search—

I have seen the wills
of two of my sixth Great-Grandfathers
One will from 1733
The other from 1755
and in these wills
both from Staten Island, New York
each man had two slaves
a man and a woman
that were willed to his family members
And it is not unrealistic to think
that these enslavers had siblings
who were also enslavers

In these DNA matches that are added to each week
some people include their portrait
and I have seen
at least a half-dozen African-Americans
appear on my list
in the category of fifth to eighth cousin
who have a small percentage of Irish
or English or German or Dutch
or another origin that is in my DNA

If you are White
and your ancestors were in this country
before to the death of slavery
you can be fairly certain
that you have Black cousins
maybe distant fifth to eighth cousins
and your ancestors need not be
from the southern states
because even the free states
were not always free

You can be fairly certain
that Whites have Black cousins
and Blacks have White cousins
but here's something else to think about—
and that is that you may look White now
or you may look Black now
but that may not have always been so

Historically speaking—
A child who was born half Black/half White
was known back then as a *"mulatto"*
and their children could become
one-quarter Black or one-quarter White
in just one generation
and their grandchildren could become
one-eighth Black or one-eighth White
in only two generations
and soon "passing" for one race or the other
(as it once was said)

Within every century
there are three to four generations
How many generations have there been
since slavery has lived here?

All I'm trying to say
(without sounding too preachy)
is try to look at a person as an individual
and not as some group you think they belong to

We all know people within our own race
who we don't like or trust
or even want to be in the same room with
but it's not because of their race
it's because of their character—
the person inside we came to know over time

And so—
for all the Whites who hate Blacks
and all the Blacks who hate Whites
who feel a deep, blind hatred
for every individual within a race
(before taking the time
for a handshake and a "Hello")—
try to keep this in mind—

we may all be cousins

## THE MAGAZINE CHALLENGE

I think we all know
that race relations in this country
aren't where they should be
and in some cases
they are moving backwards in time
and civility
I get that

But, at the same time
there has been progress made
that maybe only someone my age
someone who lived in and through those times
can see and feel

The easiest way to see that progress
is to flip through a magazine

One that was on the newsstands
prior to 1965
prior to the Civil Rights Movement

Like television of that era
magazines were predominately White—
Cover-to-cover Caucasian

The only people of color
you ever saw on television back then
was someone in a service role
A Black or Asian servant
cook or elevator operator
A Latino farmhand or bandito

So it was with the magazines at that time
Magazines with names like:
LOOK
LIFE
TIME
NEWSWEEK
The Saturday Evening Post

I can look around today
and see the progress
that people younger than I may not see

I can think back to my childhood
when you saw no person of color
being policemen
or firemen
let alone being Chief of the force
or the Mayor of a city
Congressman
Senator
Reporter
News Anchor
President—
All White

Servant roles?
Yes—
Migrant farm workers
Shoeshine boys
Gas station attendants

Of course, some inroads were made
in sports and music

You saw people like Louis Armstrong
Ella Fitzgerald and Nat King Cole
Lena Horne and Billy Holiday
Jackie Robinson and Joe Louis
Ray Charles and Harry Belafonte

There were a few Blacks
that were seen by the Media
as "safe and acceptable"
And later along came
Sammy Davis, Jr.
Mohammad Ali
Sidney Poitier
Flip Wilson
Motown

But, prior to 1965
the world
as seen through the eyes of the Media
was wall-to-wall White

If you're much younger than I
and don't see the progress
then I would suggest that you take
The Magazine Challenge

Find an old magazine somewhere
A thrift store or used book shop
Find a mainstream magazine
like LOOK, LIFE, TIME or the POST
and leaf through it

I picked up
a Saturday Evening Post the other day
from two weeks before I was born
and when I suggested this idea to my Wife
she suggested that I count up the images
Tally them up

So, I counted any image
that portrayed a person
Photograph or illustration
News item or advertisement
and found 295 images

Of those, 289 were White
3 were Black
2 were Asian
1 was a "Hindu" in a traveler's check ad
and there were no Native Americans

Of the 3 Black representations
one was a photo for a movie ad
of Louis Armstrong
to the right and in the back
behind Frank Sinatra
and other White movie stars

One was a cartoon
of the baseball player Minnie Minosa
(born in Cuba)

And one was a strange
sort of "blackface" illustration
of a woman's head
for a hair comb ad

There was a one-page news item
about Japan
with two photos of Japanese people

I guess I was a lucky kid back then
because I had an uncle who was Black
My Uncle Clarence
And I had parents
who didn't use the word *nigger*
Who sat on the couch with us boys one night
and showed us their grade school class photos
from the 1930s
when the children stood in rows
on little risers
and on the ground propped up
in front of the lowest row
was a blackboard with white letters
showing the year
grade
school
and teacher's name

My parents pointed to the rows
of Black and White kids
standing side-by-side with one another
and said: *We were all playmates*
*We all got along*
*and we saw no difference*
*whether you were Black or White*

We Shiner boys were lucky
to have parents like that

But in society and the Media
there was a big difference
between Black and White people
Especially in the southern Jim Crow states
that gave us the haunting images
of fire hoses and police dogs
and people being beaten
for sitting at a "Whites-Only" lunch counter
Lynchings
Church bombings
Burning crosses on front lawns
and signs in restaurants reading:
     *NO Dogs - Negroes - Mexicans*

And if you feel skeptical
when I say there has been progress
in race relations here in America
since the Civil Rights Movement
then I would suggest that you take
The Magazine Challenge
to see how far we've come as a society

Yes—
I see these white supremacist groups
getting attention in the Media lately
but they are a small minority
and things will never be perfect

But take The Magazine Challenge
and then look around today
at Police Officers and Firefighters
Doctors and Lawyers
Professors and Mayors
Senators and CEOs
Millionaires and Billionaires
A President whose father was African

We have a long way to go
but take The Magazine Challenge
and take a look at today
We have come a long way

## TALKING OVER BREAKFAST

I read a quote one day
of the poet William Butler Yeats
who said something like:
> *A poet cannot write*
> *as if talking to someone*
> *over breakfast*

But I would beg to differ

Being able to write
as if talking to someone over breakfast
is exactly why poets like Walt Whitman
Carl Sandburg and Charles Bukowski
were so widely read
and continue to be on the shelves of bookstores
even today, years after their deaths

Telling it like it is
No fluff
No double-meanings
No mysterious passages
Just straightforward
cut-to-the-chase honesty
as if you were sitting there
right across the table from them

And I think poetry largely lost its audience
*precisely* because poets did not write
as if they were talking to someone over breakfast

They became so esoteric and unreadable
that no one cared to read what they wrote
except other poets

(Talk about shooting yourself in the foot!)

Well—anyway—I've got to run—
But maybe we can get together
and discuss it all further sometime—
talking over breakfast

# YOU JUST NEVER KNOW

Our birthdays are not far apart
or shall I say
I was born a year and a few days earlier
which doesn't really matter
never did

The point is
whenever my birthday is approaching
I often think of Mark

We were classmates in college
18 or 19-year-olds
and later we were roommates on 7<sup>th</sup> Street
and co-workers at Dos Amigos
a Mexican restaurant
near Cass and Lake streets
It isn't there anymore
but we were dos amigos
who worked at Dos Amigos

Last week I was in the kitchen
looking at the calendar on the wall
mentioning to Jan
that my old roommate Mark
would be having a birthday
right about now
but that I couldn't quite pinpoint the date

I wondered what he might be up to now
and thought, for some reason
that he may still be living in or near
the town where we lived and worked
and went to college in

So, I went to the laptop on the kitchen table
and typed in his name and the city
and up came an obituary—
Dammit!

I read the glowing account
of the man in the obituary
which left no doubt
that it was the same Mark I know
(or had once known)

Besides the familiar names and places mentioned
there was the description of an adventurous man
who loved the great outdoors
who loved music
who was a loving husband
who was the friend who would stay up all night
and listen to you when you needed it
who always left his door open
Yeah—
that was Mark

He had passed away four years earlier
just past his 62nd birthday
Dammit!

And the writer (I'm guessing his wife)
may have meant it figuratively
that he always left his door open
but I do recall
that the apartment we lived in on 7th Street
always had an open door— literally
or at least an unlocked door—
None of us had a key to it
Not Mark or I
or any of the third roommates
who we tried from time to time
to make monthly rent easier
But the third roommates
never seemed to work out—
Anyway—
the door was always open
No one had a key

I worked the evening shift
and some nights

I never knew who might be there
when I walked in the door after midnight

One night I walked in
and sitting out in the kitchen
was a stranger, alone
with a pint of Irish whiskey in front of him
He took a sip and said
> *Hi, I'm a friend of Mark's*
> *My name is Dolomite*
Doe-lo-mite? I asked
> *Yeah, Dolomite*
OK, well, I'm Jack

And we sat and talked in the kitchen for a while
when suddenly there were footsteps on the stairs
running up quickly
The door flew open
and a young woman came running in
(Well, we were all young then)
and she ran into the living room
sees us out in the kitchen
and says
> *Ya gotta hide me!*
with desperation in her voice
and a bicycle lock and chain held in one hand
OK—
She has my attention—
So, I ask what the story is
and why the lock and chain?
She says she was walking down the street
when some guys in a pickup truck
started harassing her
She says she took a swing
and clocked one of the guys in the face with the lock
took off running
and came here because she heard
it was cool to come here

Rrrreal-ly? I said, (sounding somewhat surprised)
Wow!— Did these guys see you come here?

She says
>*No..... I don't think so*
>*but ya gotta hide me*
>*Can I crash here for the night?*

I said, Yeah, I guess—
You can crash on the couch over there
>*Oh, thanks... yeah, thanks... she says*

Dolomite left with his pint of whiskey
and I would see him around town
from time to time
but when I woke the next day
and walked out into the living room
the young woman was gone
and I never saw her again
One strange night

Somehow
word got around
that it was cool to hang out at our place
and one night I was sitting in my room
quietly strumming guitar after work
when I hear voices in the living room
I look out my bedroom door
and there's four guys I've never seen before
sitting and talking like they own the place
I walk out and say, Hey, what's up?
>*Oh, we heard it was cool to hang out for a while*

I said, Well, ya have to keep it down
My roommate's right in that room
and he needs to get up and work a day shift
>*Oh, yeah, cool, we'll keep it down*

But then
not only did the talking start up again
but they all started singing the chorus to the song
>*Papa was a Rolling Stone*

and started play fighting
Just horsing around
Nothing serious or violent
but noisy

So, I went back into the living room and said
        Hey, guys, ya gotta keep it down
They ended up leaving
and I never saw any of them again
Another strange night
and there were a few strange nights

Anyway—
I remember the place
and the time I spent there
It was back in the middle of The Seventies
Both Mark and I had hair below our shoulders
both played guitar and had liberal politics
if any
We had no TV or telephone
and we were both OK with that
Music
Reading
Talk
We were OK with that as entertainment

Mark worked the day shift at Dos Amigos
and I went in at 3pm and got off at midnight
The owners, Dave and Claudia
were sweethearts to work for
Like family
They wanted us to eat after we clocked in
and again before we clocked out
So, we pretty much lived on burritos
tostadas, tacos and nachos
Life was good

I would use the pay phone over on Union Street
and was talking to my brother George
who said he could get me a job
at a factory he was working in
down in suburban Detroit
I said— *Nah, I don't wanna work in a factory again*
He told me what the pay would be
I said— *I'll be there Monday*

And these were the days
before the Internet and email
before cell phones and texting
before social media
and there was no phone in the apartment
So, after I left to go downstate
to work my last factory job
Mark and I lost touch with one another

It was easier to lose touch back then

And time goes by
and life moves on
and you think:
> *Wow, it's been more than 40 years*
> *I wonder what my old friend is up to now*
and dammit— you find an obituary

And you also find some memories
still tucked away on your back pages...
I still recall those times
with Mark and Becky
Jeff, Ted, Scott, Tom, Leslie, Dolomite
and others whose names
I can't come up with right now
and I even remember some of the faces
of those neither of us knew
who may appear through the open door
of our apartment one night
disappear
and never be seen again

The door was always open
or at least unlocked

And sometimes life
knocks you back a step
with an unexpected moment
like trying to look up an old friend
and finding an obituary
and what do you do with that?

What can you do with that?

Except to say—
Mark— you got ripped off, man
You got a few decades stolen from you
and the world's a lesser place
without someone like you in it

Rest in Peace, Mark

Rest in Peace, old friend
and maybe find that key
and lock the door, once in a while
because you just never know, man

You just never know

# I TRULY DO

I wish all the unborn well
I truly do
But I also worry about the world
and the conditions awaiting the unborn
physically
environmentally
politically
culturally

I also worry about some of the lawmakers
mostly men
who have no medical background
who seem to have very little empathy
who seem to think those nine months
are little more than a round of golf
and who seem to think very little
about what happens after those nine months

I worry about those who continue their push
to make all abortions illegal in this country
Illegal regardless of rape and incest
regardless of the condition of the fetus
regardless of the condition of the mother

Those who want every fetus born
without considering the child
and the quality of life that child will have
Will it be unwanted, neglected, and abused?
Will it be unstable?
Will it be unable to live a normal life
due to catastrophic physical defects?

And my question to these lawmakers
and anyone who supports
making all abortions illegal is this:
How many unwanted children have you adopted?
How many neglected, abused, unstable children?
How many unable to lead a normal life?

And if your mind is reeling
while reaching for reasons why you haven't—
then let me ask you this:
How many unwanted children
will you promise to adopt
at this very moment?
Right now

It seems that a great deal of action
is given to the issue
of seeing the fetus through to birth

and then—
once the child is born—

all goes silent—

The action ceases—

Any talk becomes lip service

Any support disappears

And there are no promises kept—
because there were no promises made

I wish all the unborn well—

　　　I truly do

## GRASS FIRES

Rumors—
Most travel as fast as a summer grass fire
and are about as useless

In a small town
rumors can become the news
because in a small town
there's never enough news to consume
So, a certain percentage of it
needs to be created

I recall when I was living
in a small town of six hundred people
I worked at one of the two bars in town
Two bars on one street
Two bars facing each other
on opposite sides of Waukazoo Street

It was called the Hotel Northern
but all the locals called it
    The Hotel Liquor
because of the red neon sign
above the side entrance that read:
**HOTEL**
**LIQUOR**

One summer day
A slow afternoon
A few of the locals
Fairly quiet
when through the front door
Rosie comes bursting in
rushing over to the end of the bar
where I stood leaning on it
resting on an elbow

With a wild look of concern
she grabs both of my arms
shakes me and says:

*YOU'RE ALIVE!*

I say, *Of course I am*

*YOU'RE ALIVE!* she continues—
*Oh! Thank God! You're alive!*
*It's all over town that you were killed*
*in a motorcycle accident!*

*But—* I say
*I don't even own a motorcycle*

The bar became fairly quiet again

Rosie went out the front door
I assume to spread the news all over town
that I was indeed alive and well
and didn't even own a motorcycle

And I would guess that all the excitement
died down for a while
or at least until another grass fire was set ablaze
to torch the town
once more

## MAYBE IT'S JUST ME

Oh—
my—
Gawd!—
Christmas again?!!

It doesn't seem so much fun anymore
(At this age, anyway)
At this age
you are mainly thinking
of the years passing rapidly by
and the unpaid balances
still due from last Christmas
But what is probably worse than all that
is the music

Now— right there
you may have already thrown up your hands
and said: "*What a humbug he is!
A regular Ebenezer Scrooge!*"
But hear me out—
It's the same old stuff
year after year
Some of it *really* awful
and as each year passes by
the stores push the Christmas season
earlier and earlier
so that you're beginning to hear
Christmas music before Halloween!

Now, I may have mentioned this before
but I actually received
an offer in the mail this year
to purchase Christmas ornaments
in APRIL!!!
APRIL! FOR CRYIN' OUT LOUD!
APRIL?
C'MON!

As I write this

it is late November
Christmas music is expected then
But, yesterday
I had the unfortunate experience
of having to sit through the song
"Felice Navidad"
Twice!
Twice, mind you!
And that right there
is a loose definition of what it means
to spend eternity in Hell!

Believe me—
if you ever think there is some information
that I am withholding from you
I'll make the extraction of said information
very easy for you to get out of me—
Just tie me to a chair
and begin to play two Christmas songs:
the ever repetitious "Felice Navidad"
and the evermore repetitious
and even more dreadful
"Twelve Days of Christmas"
(Five GOLD-en Rrrrrrrings)

Believe me
before you get through each song twice
I'll spill my guts
Anything!
I'll tell you anything you want to hear!
Just turn it off!
PLEASE just turn it off!
Anything!
(Five GOLD-en Rrrrrrrings)
NO! NO! NO!
ANYTHING!
And all of it the truth
I promise
I promise
Please— I beg you
JUST TURN IT OFF!

*Joy To The World?*
Yes, yes, yes
at least that one is musical
  *Silent Night?*
OK, yes
touching in its solemn way
But some of the others
you can just pitch out the window
with last night's dishwater
and this year's gift wrappings

Maybe we should take the title
of the Twelve Days of Christmas
literally
and pass a national law
limiting the Christmas season to twelve days
Only twelve days
I mean—
at some point someone has to put a lid on it
don't you think?
I suppose if we don't
we'll be singing *Jingle Bells*
at the Fourth of July picnic!
For cryin' out loud!

That's it!
Enough!
Twelve days - December 14th through the 25th
Count them
Yes, twelve days
And jack-booted thugs
patrolling the streets to enforce it
and if any store dares to play a Christmas song
through their overhead speakers
or in the elevators
before December 14th
their front doors will be chained and padlocked
until the day after Christmas

No first offense warnings
No negotiations— No!

Padlocks and chains
Zero tolerance
Sorry
You play—
You pay!

And radio stations—
Same rules
No Christmas music before December 14<sup>th</sup>
and on top of that
public service announcements to warn us
when they are about to broadcast
the *really* awful ones

> *This is your two-minute warning*
> *Please turn your volume down*
> *or leave the premises*
> *we are about to broadcast*
> *the Twelve Days of Christmas*

Suddenly
from storefronts all over the city
droves of citizens flock to the streets
hands over their ears
>    *NO! NO!*
>    *NOT THE FIVE GOLDEN RINGS!!!*

or
maybe it's just me

## RAGGED LITTLE SQUARES

Years ago
I read a quote of Beethoven
that had something to do
with you realizing
how far you have progressed
by how much you dislike
your earlier works

It makes me think back to a time
when I was in my late twenties
sitting in my studio apartment
where I lived in San Francisco

That particular evening
I had gotten out
all my binders of poetry
and sat on the floor
with them laying all around me

I had developed the meticulous habit
of placing all my poems in 3-ring binders
in chronological order
and I looked at them all
got up
took a few steps to the little kitchen
in the corner of the room
came back with a brown paper bag
opened it
and began pulling poems from the binders
and ripping them up
into ragged little squares
about a ragged little inch or so
on each side

In a rage?
No
I would say if anything
it was caused by discomfort

I had been keeping
everything I had written
since the age of fourteen
when I felt that it all
should be chiseled into marble
But now—
I sat there on the floor
looking at the sameness of it all
the dullness of it
the feebleness of it
and decided that there were some layers of skin
that needed to be shed

Had I lived in an apartment with a fireplace
I think it would have been fitting
for it all to go up in smoke
But—
as I did not have a fireplace
a brown paper bag would have to do

I kept a decent example here and there
and ripped up all the similar ones
into ragged little squares
tossing them into the bag

And by the end of the evening
the bag was almost half full—
almost half full of ragged little squares
with fragments of thoughts
bits of ideas
pieces of yesterday

My younger self
would have sat there in shock
mouth agape
arms outstretched with clenched fists
shouting:
*What are you doing?!!*
*How is the World ever going to recover*
*from such a loss as this?!!*

But my new self would say:

*Relax, young one*
*There is no need for recovery*
*for there has been no loss*

*What you see there in that bag*
*half full of ragged little squares*
*is not a loss*
*nor wasted years*
*What you see there*
*is a new beginning*

# NEVER GIVE UP

Poets are the dust
   swept under the rug of society

You are the bottom rung
   on the literary ladder

More people read smut
   than poetry

So—
   get used to it

Just keep writing—

   and never give up

## POETIC ADVICE

Try—
once in a while—
to sneak in a little time
to write a poem while you're at work—
on the clock

It may very well be
    the only possible way
        you'll ever get paid for doing so

## WHERE DO I BEGIN?

Hmmmm—
Where do I begin with this one?

We Americans
have got some things
deeply ingrained in our minds
that are wrong
or, at least, only partially right
and it is not our fault
and it is our fault at the same time
So—
let the confusion begin

I say it is not our fault
because it is what we are taught
from a young age in our schools
and reinforced annually by our media

I say it is our fault
because we generally do not read
research
explore
question
or search for the truth ourselves

For example—
consider this:
The day I write this is September 4th
one day after
the 240th anniversary of the independence
of the United States of America

And you say:
*Oh, no, no, no, partner—*
*You got that all wrong*
*You mean July 4th*
*July 4th 1776*
*That's Independence Day*
*It always has been*

*You know—*
*flag waving and parades*
*backyard bar-b-ques*

And yeah
I know what we've been taught—
but the British
still occupied the colonies of New York
South Carolina and Georgia in 1782
and the Treaty of Peace with England
wasn't signed until September 3rd 1783
That's when England
formally recognized the independence
of the United States of America
Two years after Cornwallis
surrendered to Washington at Yorktown

We seem to have it ingrained in our minds
that it was on July 4th 1776
we became the United States of America
Independent
Instantly
Game over
Done deal

Not quite
Not even close, really—
and I don't mean to bombard you
with a deluge of detail and data
but nothing was a done deal at all

John Adams
who was later our first Vice President
and then our second President
wrote that at the time of the Revolution
(that was then simply called *The Cause*)
one third of the population were in favor
one third were loyal to the King and against it
and one third were indifferent

Benjamin Franklin was in the thick of it all

but he was in Europe
for 24 of the 28 years between 1757 and 1785
as an agent for the Pennsylvania colony
as well as a Peace Commissioner
in the latter years of his stay

In February of 1775
the House of Commons in Parliament
moved to declare the colony
of Massachusetts in rebellion
not the entire 13 colonies
That was the result of what we know
as The Boston Tea Party

Benjamin Franklin was informed by the British
that the Continental Congress
should pay for the tea destroyed in Boston Harbor

Franklin replied
that Massachusetts alone should pay
not all the colonies
So, things were not united—
quite yet

The colonies saw themselves
as individual republics
Each with their own governments
their own militias
The people did not think of themselves
as being from one nation

When they spoke of their "country"
they meant Virginia
or Pennsylvania
New York
The colony where they were born and lived
that was their "country"

The Coercive Acts passed by Parliament
were aimed at the Massachusetts colony
and Boston Harbor

It was to order Boston Harbor closed
until the destroyed tea was paid for

Then came the acts
to dissolve the Massachusetts government
to declare a Royal Governor
who would then appoint members to council
There would be no elections
The Governor would appoint Judges
and no town meetings could take place
without the Royal Governor's approval

In London they thought
that when the other 12 colonies
learned of this
they would fall in line
and do their duty as loyal subjects—
Of this they were mistaken

The colonies did unite—
to embargo both imports and exports of England
And the Merchant class
particularly in England
was not very happy about this
The economy spiraled downward
People lost work
Some businesses were shuttered
things came to a head

When the battles started
there were problems on both sides
and the biggest problem for the British Generals
was that reinforcements
were over 3,000 miles across the Atlantic Ocean

One badly chosen battle
could cripple the mission
and by the time your reports
reached your commanders in London
it could be months before you heard any reply
and your situation could be entirely changed

and their new orders entirely unsuited
to the current conditions
Complete chaos

Another thing about all this
is that we Americans
tend to have the impression
that the American Revolution
was all that was happening at the time
when in reality
there was a global war going on
between England, France,
Spain and the Netherlands
The colonies were only one of the worries

In the beginning
the British thought that one battle
one good slap on the face
would put the colonies in line
and they could get back to the global war
but some good sharp slaps
were landing on the British as well
and as the Revolutionary War dragged on
the Merchant class
and the Government class in London
were tired of the expense
and felt that fighting the French
in the West Indies
would be a better use of finances
which was a strategic reason
for still occupying New York
South Carolina and Georgia

New York for its harbor
and strategic place in the Atlantic

South Carolina and Georgia
as bases from which
to launch attacks on the French
and focus on the Caribbean theatre
The West Indies had to be protected

The contest with America
had become a secondary matter

And then there was King George III
who just did not want to give in
But—
Anyway—
I didn't mean for this poem
to drag on and on

It was just meant to be an example
to illustrate the fact
that we are sometimes only given a headline
instead of the whole story
and even the headline
may need to be fact-checked

I think you know some of what I'm talking about:
That Washington chopped down a cherry tree
and never told a lie
for instance

And what about Johnny Appleseed
who we learned had traipsed about
planting apple trees with a tin pot on his head?
But we come to find out
that the variety he was planting
wasn't edible for eating
It was a variety for making hard cider
So, what's up with that?

Let me just lay it out from what I have read:
On July 2nd Congress voted 12-0
to approve to *declare* independence

On July 4th
the declaration was sent to a printer
who put that date on the document

On July 9th
New York made the vote unanimous at 13-0

On August 2<sup>nd</sup>
most of the delegates
put their signatures on the document

During this time period
British General Howe had landed on Staten Island
with 9,000 troops
and shortly thereafter
his brother Admiral Howe arrived
with a fleet of more than 200 ships

To declare independence was one thing
To gain independence was quite another
and that independence was not recognized
until September 3<sup>rd</sup> 1783
when John Adams, Benjamin Franklin and John Jay
signed the Treaty of Peace with England in Paris
with which England recognized
the Independence of the United States of America

A few days later, Franklin wrote:
> *"May we never see another war*
> *for in my opinion*
> *there has never been a good war*
> *or a bad peace"*

Oh, where do I begin?

## TINY

Redwood trees
fading into the fog

Few sights are as stately
as redwoods fading into the fog
Their gentle green and soft brown colors
fading into the blues and grays
of the mist that enshrouds them

Some of them 300 feet high
and 22 feet wide
with long memories
Some 2,000 years old

These trees remember DaVinci
as if it were yesterday
The American Revolution
was just a wink ago
to these tall time travelers

Respect them
They deserve it
They've been around the block
a time or two

That tiny seed
and 2,000 years of sunlight
moisture and soil

That tiny miraculous seed

# TOTALITY

In search of the path of totality
we travel south from Michigan
and then southwest
into the lower regions of Illinois

The media has been saying for weeks
that Carbondale is the place to go
So, that is exactly where I don't want to be

I study the predicted path of totality
and decide on a location
southeast of Carbondale
near a dot on the map marked Bloomfield
but Jan and I never find Bloomfield
or we passed it by
(without realizing it was a town)
and beneath Interstate 24 we go
where we end up in a town called Vienna
which the locals don't pronounce as VEE-enna
but say VY-enna instead

There are still about thirty minutes
before the solar eclipse begins

Jan and I tour the town
and find the Johnson County Courthouse
with its park-like grounds
Trees for shade in the 90-degree humid heat
OK
This is the place

We backtrack to the town's grocery store
for sandwiches and potato salad
and before the eclipse begins
we have a picnic lunch
on the old Courthouse grounds

As we eat, I take a glimpse
through the dark sunglasses

94

and see that the Moon
has had a bite of the sun
There are twenty minutes left to totality

Little groups gather on the lawns
Some with cameras and telescopes
but most
like us
with only our eclipse sunglasses

We eat our sandwiches
potato salad and apples
and periodically check the progress
of the Sun and the Moon

I text my son Frank and brother George
who are both experiencing it in Oregon
They say it was amazing
Beyond imagination
    Wait—
    It happened for you already?
Yes, at 10:19am

For us in southern Illinois
it had not happened yet
but the light was getting dimmer
as crescent shapes began to appear
in the shadows of branches
The clouds were cooperating
so far

Just a sliver of light left—
And as it began to get quite dim
a loud choir of insects
began to sound in the trees
It seemed to all of them
that dusk was approaching
and it was time for their nightly performance

They got louder
and then someone shouted *THERE IT IS!*

I removed my eclipse glasses
and there in the sky it was
The Corona
fluttering around the deep gray of the Moon
Stars appeared
as a shout and a holler rose collectively
from those of us
craning our necks
looking almost directly above
with gasps of
>        *WOW!*
>        *AMAZING!*
>        *SPEC-TAC-U-LAR!*

as surrounding clouds appeared to be backlit
with twilight colors
from the light outside of the Umbra

The loud insect chorus continued
for two and a half minutes
and then just a pinprick of the Sun reappeared
and it was too bright
to look up at the Sun any longer
The eclipse glasses had to go back on
and the immediate thought at that moment was:
>        *NO*
>        *Please don't go*
>        *Come back*
>        *I want to see more of that*
>        *I want to see it again*
>        *When and where is the next one?*

And as the dimness changed
to full daylight once again
the insects settled back to silence
as we onlookers were still walking around
with smiles on our faces
and as we onlookers were about to learn a lesson
about viewing a total eclipse:
>        Never try to leave the area
>        of the total eclipse on the same day—
>        Never!

I-24 and I-57 were at a crawl
Five miles per hour
and all the secondary roads were the same
Thirty minutes or more
just to get up an on-ramp
and to the point of merging into the mayhem

The 50 was twenty miles to the north
but at this rate
it was going to take four hours to get there
with everyone from northern Illinois
Chicago and Wisconsin
crawling up I-57

We had to abort—
and find another path to Michigan
Northeast to Indianapolis
and then north
except—
there was a problem—
Everyone from Indiana
was trying to get back on I-64 and I-69
So, what should have taken
five and a half hours to get to Michigan
became twelve hours

Meanwhile—
out in Oregon
it took George, Karen, and Frank
five hours to cover the thirty-five miles
they needed to travel home

But—
it was worth it!

Put it on your list of "Must Do" within your lifetime
But—
don't try to leave the area on the same day
Seriously—
you can totally trust me on that one

## THE RED PADDLE

The device of downright discipline
The means of muffling mischievous mayhem
The contraption of corrective condemnation
The bottom warmer of boisterous rambunctious boys
That regulator of authority
    also known as—
        The Red Paddle

Oh, to hear those words
within a phrase or a sentence
would widen the eyes
make your blood run cold
the hair on the back of your neck stand up
and make you stop in your tracks
looking for the nearest escape route

Mom's voice:
    *I'M GOING TO GET THE RED PADDLE!!!*

All four of us boys—
stopping in our tracks
looking around at one another
      *Oh-oh!*
    *The Red Paddle!*
      *Boy, you're gonna get it!*
    *Whaddya mean me?*
      *You did it!*
    *Did not!*
      *Did too, ya big brown butthole!*
    *Did not neither... he did*
        *Me? MOM— THEY'RE BLAMING ME!*

And then the ominous sound
of the drawer sliding open—
    The Dreaded Drawer of Doom
out in the otherwise cozy kitchen
    Home of—
        The Red Paddle

And off we boys would scatter
but there weren't too many places to run and hide
in that little nine-hundred square foot house

The kitchen?
No way!
That's where she is
with a firm grip on The Red Paddle
and the fierce and determined look of
    *You're gonna get it!*
blazing in her beautiful blue eyes

The dining room?
Are you kidding?
She'll be in there next
as she makes her way
to the scene of the latest crime
created by the Kids of Chaos

The bathroom?
Not a chance!
There's nowhere to hide in there
but we could get under the beds
or in the closet
if we can make it to the bedroom fast enough

*Boy, oh boy!*
    *We gotta get outta here!*
*She can make it out of the kitchen*
*and through the dining room*
*before ya know it!*
    *Not much time now!*
*What are we gonna do?*
    *Quick! Behind the chair!*
(Not enough room for all of us there
so... someone is going to get pushed
right out into the open)

*Gee whiz!*
    *RUN FOR YOUR LIFE!!!*
    *IT'S THE RED PADDLE!!!*

And now—
I think it just and prudent
to pause here for a moment
to clear the good name of my Mother
because— after all
we boisterous rambunctious boys
deserved each and every searing smack
our bottoms received from The Red Paddle

It's not as if it was a surprise to us
We knew we had it coming
You'd think we would have learned
from past experience
but no—
that would have required
a modicum of logic and reasonable deduction
and we all knew that anything like that
would just get in the way
of all the fun we were having
So, we'd throw caution to the wind
and continue to create a chaos
of our own special brand
brought to you by:
    Shiner Brothers Kid Chaos Incorporated
         (Patent pending)

And in the midst of the chaos
if something got broken
or something went wildly wrong
we went dead silent—
whispering what to do
or where to hide it
and then the silence would be broken
by Mom calling out from another room
    *WHAT DID YOU BOYS DO NOW?*

*Holy Moley!*
    *How the heck does she know already?*
*Does she have a camera in every room?*
    *How do Moms do that?*

Then she would appear in the doorway
hands on her hips
looking at what we'd done
or were trying to hide
and say:
    *Well, isn't THAT just DUCKY?*

Somehow *Ducky*
was not a good thing to be—
We could figure that much out
and we also knew that *Ducky*
was only the First Level of
    The Red Paddle Alert
We all knew that The Red Paddle
was still a long way off
if we could keep the situation
contained at the *Ducky* level
But what were the chances of that?
Slim to none
when the Shiner Boys were involved!

When she disappeared from the doorway
the silence would soon be shattered
as we revved it all back up
to a raucous roar
until such time when we heard
the Second Level of The Red Paddle Alert
which sounded something like this:
    *JESUS CHRIST ALMIGHTY!!!*

Hoo boy!
Now things were getting a bit risky
A bit dangerous and dicey
because sometimes the Second Level Alert
was enough to bring out The Red Paddle
and I guess that sort of depended
on how many First Level Ducky Alerts
you already chalked up that day
and we were never clever enough to count those—
but one good
    *JESUS CHRIST ALMIGHTY!!!*

was enough to perk up your ears
to listen for the sound of
    The Dreaded Drawer of Doom

If we didn't hear the drawer slide open
we knew we still had a chance
or, at least, maybe a chance
to keep it to a Second Level Alert
We knew the Ducky phase was over
Ka-put!
No chance of a Ducky phase returning
for another 24 hours
at least

Nope
Now what we had here
was a Second Level Alert on our hands
and Second Level Alerts could be hard to read
Second Level Alerts
could sometimes come with a short fuse
which
again
I think depended on how many Ducky Alerts
you had already chalked up that day

And— of course—
it was inevitable
Automatically destined
It was in the cards
Bound to happen
In the bag and out of our hands
It was undeniably indisputable
and unquestionably inescapable
and just as plain as the nose on your face
that we boys were going to find a way
to light that fuse
and find out just how short it was

And you usually found that spark
in George's eyes—

Now—
I'm not saying it was always him
but I am saying
that you could usually count on George

You can still see it
in almost every photograph of him
from that time period
In color or black and white
You see the smirk
You see the gears turning
and the eyes narrowing
with a little spark
right there in the corner of his eye
Just enough of a spark
to get a short fuse fizzing

And whether it was his spark
or one of us other boys
it just plain didn't matter
because we never once
saw a short fuse that was a dud
Uh-uh
No way
Once the fizzing started
the Third and Final stage of The Red Paddle Alert
was soon to arrive
in the form of lightning and rolling thunder
The floors rumbling
and the walls shaking to the sound of:
    *YOU LITTLE SHITS!!!*

Oh, boy—
it was coming out now!
No question about that!
You may as well ask if the sky is blue
or is water wet
or does a chicken have lips

Some of the neighborhood kids might say
    *You're in Dutch now!*

or some might say
    *You're in for a whuppin'*
But we knew what we were in for:
A meeting with Destiny!
A meeting with The Red Paddle!

Because there's no way out of it now—

You're trapped
Cornered
Back to the wall
Up a tree without a ladder
In a jam and a tight spot
Up to your neck in hot water
and yes—
you *are* up a creek—
but in this case...
                    there is a paddle—

That ghastly, grim, gruesome
terrifyingly frightful
revoltingly repugnant
nightmare of your angelic childhood:

# THE RED PADDLE!!!

# NO, MAYBE NOT

When I was very young
five or six years-old maybe
I thought I would like to be a Flagman
on a road construction crew

I thought that might be the job for me
Working outside all day
No heavy lifting
You got to have that STOP/SLOW sign
on a pole or a handle
and sometimes a radio to talk into
All that—
plus— the power to stop traffic!
YES!
For a six-year-old boy
that seemed like the ideal job to me

But then a few years passed by
My horizons broadened
and by the age of eight
I had abandoned my idea of being a Flagman
and thought maybe I should be President
Yeah—
President of the United States of America
Commander in Chief

But then several decades passed
and along came The Orange One to prove me wrong

No—
maybe an eight-year-old
shouldn't be President of the United States
Commander in Chief
No—maybe not

## DEATH DOESN'T HEAL

Somebody help me here—
I am not a lawyer
I am not privy to all the details
or the technicalities
but common sense tells me
that something stinks here

Here's what I know
at the moment I write this:
A seventeen-year-old boy
travels across state lines
with an AR-15 assault rifle
carrying it in the open—
loaded—
at a protest gathering

In the midst of this
he kills two people and maims a third
yet the seventeen-year-old boy
is found Not Guilty of all charges

And I have a few questions:
How does a society allow this to happen?
What was an underage kid
doing with a killing machine like that?
A gun illegal for him to own
in his home state of Illinois
but legal for him to "open carry"
in the state of Wisconsin
according to a stretched interpretation of the law
by the sitting Judge

Apparently—
(as the law is written)
in Wisconsin it is permissible
for sixteen and seventeen-year-olds
to open carry "long rifles"
The intent of the provision
is to allow sons and daughters

to hunt with their parents
but since the intent was not specified
in the law as such
the Judge ruled that the AR-15 is a "long rifle"
and therefore, legal to open carry
loaded
on the streets of a community
during a protest gathering

But
if he had not been allowed
to open carry a loaded AR-15
would it have maybe resulted in a fist fight?
Maybe some heated words?
Maybe nothing at all?

The boy says
he was "protecting" a car dealership
(In a state he doesn't live in?)
and murdered in self-defense
because someone was chasing him
and tried to take away his gun
OK—
So, again, I ask
What was an underage kid
doing with a killing machine like that
open carrying in public
loaded
on the streets of a community
during a protest gathering?

The two people he murdered
can no longer speak for themselves
but others involved in the chase
say they were doing so
because they felt a threat of harm
to themselves and to others
if this kid opened fire

The maimed individual
apparently was pointing a handgun at the kid

So, why was that guy carrying a gun too?
Is anyone learning a lesson here?

Have we lost our sense of balance?
Have we lost our minds?
Have we lost what it means
to be a civil society?
Is there no common sense in the Justice System?
Is the system just a money-making sham?

I heard a former prosecutor say
that the law is the law
and if there was "reasonable doubt"
then the jury did the right thing

He also brought up
that the situation may have been provoked
by the seventeen-year-old boy
open carrying an assault rifle
but if a Wisconsin Judge allows it
then it's the law that needs to be changed
not the jury's verdict

And already
some people are making a folk-hero
of this teenage murderer
A former reality show President
congratulates him publicly
A Congressman of questionable judgment
offers him a congressional internship
An aging rock 'n' roller
offers him a lifetime supply of ammunition
Really?

As I see it
the root cause of the murders
is that a seventeen-year-old kid
was allowed to open carry
a loaded assault rifle on a city street
during a protest gathering

Is this what we want?
Teenagers or anyone
roaming the streets with loaded weapons
deciding that they
are going to "protect" the community?
One they may not even live in?

And five days later
down in Georgia
a Guilty verdict is passed down
to three White men
who chased down a young Black man
who was jogging in their neighborhood
and shot him dead with a shotgun

A father
son
and their neighbor

The son pulled the trigger
claiming in court
that the murder was done in self-defense
while the three of them
were attempting a "citizen's arrest"
on the unarmed jogger

Cell phone video surfaced
The three are found Guilty
And again, it's a gun
A shotgun in a pickup truck—
Loaded
In a residential neighborhood
with an irresponsible
and some might say irrational gun owner

I don't understand

Are these the communities
we want to live in?

I'm sure these three men

now wish they hadn't had a gun with them
as they sit in jail
waiting to go to prison
thinking about that split second
the gun went off
and the jogger went down
Wishing they could have that split second back
and handle the situation differently

If there had been no gun
what would have happened?
Maybe heated words?
Maybe a fist fight?
Three against one?
Maybe nothing?

Words can be forgotten
or apologized for
Bruises can fade—
but death doesn't heal

And with a gun—
one bad decision and a split second
changes everything
forever

And I'm sure these three men
are thinking about that split second
over and over again
as they sit in jail
waiting to go to prison
perhaps for decades
perhaps for the rest of their lives

Thinking about their lives ahead
and what will happen to their families outside
as they sit inside prison
year after year after wasted year
because of one bad decision
and a split second
that wasted the life of an unarmed jogger

His life gone
What about his family?

Heated words?
You could say
      *"Sorry about that"* and shake hands
Bloody noses and bruises
aren't a way to handle it either
but at least you could say
      *"Hey, sorry, man*
       *I don't know what I was thinking"*
But death doesn't heal
and saying
      *"Sorry about that*
       *I don't know what I was thinking"*
isn't going to cut it
on any level imaginable

And I hope the seventeen-year-old kid
with the AR-15
thinks about these things too
because he is free to open carry
and kill again

Do we really want our communities to be like this?

And—
Aww, C'mon!!!
I would like to finish this poem
but now a fifteen-year-old kid
has killed four classmates
and wounded seven others
in my home state of Michigan
with a 9mm handgun
that his father had purchased for him
just a few days earlier
AS A CHRISTMAS GIFT!!!

A 9mm handgun
for a fifteen-year-old kid
as a Christmas gift?

Really?

Did this father
have the gun secured in a gun safe
only to be brought out for target practice
under adult supervision?
Obviously not!

Four teenagers dead and seven others wounded
on the same day that both parents
were called into the school office
and told that they must get their child
psychiatric help within 48 hours
for the behavior he had been displaying

48 hours too late—
as one report suggested that the handgun
was in the child's backpack
as he left the office and went back to class

Later that same day
the news of an "active shooter" at the high school
flashes throughout the community

The mother sends a text to her son
        *Ethan, don't do it*
A little too late, Mom

The dad calls 911
to report a gun missing from his house
or—
did he know that gun
was in the child's backpack?

Details surface
that a few days earlier
a teacher reported to higher-ups
that the child was in class
searching for places to buy ammo
on his cell phone

The parents were alerted to this
and the mother sent her son
the following text:
>  *LOL – I'm not mad at you*
>  *You have to learn*
>  *how not to get caught*

The parents did not appear
at their scheduled arraignment
A manhunt begins
and finds them hiding in an empty art studio
in a warehouse down in Detroit
They are arrested and charged

Their attorney tried to spin it
by saying that they were not hiding
they were "sequestering" themselves to be safe
Nice try—
The Sheriff isn't buying it
and I don't think a Judge or jury will either

A 9mm handgun
as a Christmas gift for a fifteen-year-old
Bad decision, Dad
And how do you feel now, Mom
about supporting that decision?
I suspect you'll both have prison time
to think about this

To the gun owners who own guns
to go hunting or target practice safely
or have a gun inside their home
for home protection—
I understand that

But the parents who buy their children guns
and the gun owners
who open carry weapons outside their homes
and into the community
with some idea in their heads
that they have the authority

to be Officer, Judge and Jury—
        they are all dangerous—
                and need to be dealt with—

Period

They have already made a bad decision
        for themselves
                and the rest of us

One bad decision
        and a split second—

                Death—
                        doesn't heal

# WITH NO REGRETS

Bald—
Bald for several years now
Completely shaved bald with a goatee

As a teenager
I would have *never* imagined
this happening to me
Never!

In the late Sixties and early Seventies
for a guy to grow his hair out
was a cool thing
It was different
Long
below the ears
below the shoulders
halfway down your back
(if you could get away with it)

After all—
you did have your parents to deal with
and their generation saw it as sloppy
unkempt
feminine
or rebellious

We young guys
saw it as rebellious too
As being ourselves
Standing out from the norm
and *Cool, man, cool!*

But it was a rough road getting there

My oldest brother Rick was the first to try
and every night at the dinner table
Mom and Dad would be harassing him
to cut his hair (and get a job)

I was about fourteen
when I first started refusing to get haircuts
My brother George was sixteen
and my brother Keith was twelve

I was sitting on the front porch one day
when out of the front door came my Dad
who walked a protesting Keith
to the top of the porch steps
and gave him a kick in the butt
that launched him down to the lawn
saying:
*And don't come back until you have a haircut!*

I was about fifteen when I experienced
the weirdest morning of my life—
I opened my eyes upon awakening
and there was my mother's face
about one foot away from mine
smiling
saying nothing
just smiling and holding her hand out
palm up
with candy in it

In this awkward moment
I was trying to adjust to reality
when my brother Keith burst into the room
his hair all hacked up and yelled
   *RUN!*
   *JUST GET UP AND RUN, MAN!*
   *SHE'S GOING TO BUTCHER YOUR HAIR!!!*

And— she did

It was the last haircut I got
until I was out of high school

The parents gave up and gave in
and all four of us brothers grew our hair out long
down our backs

and tied it back like colonial Americans
or salty sailors of old

I had my long hair and ponytail
on and off throughout my life
depending on what type of job I had

I grew it out again when I was forty-five
and kept a ponytail until I was sixty-one

By that time
I only had a wreath of white-gray on the sides
bald on top and in the back
and a thin ponytail about a foot long

I gave up—
If I was going to be bald
I was going to be bald all the way
and I did so

And you discover a few things when you do so
such as
you can't hold a pencil behind your ear anymore
and the rain runs down your face
unless you have a hat on
There's nothing up there
to hold the rain back anymore
But you also won't have a "bad hair day"
No need to buy shampoo
Nothing to put on or in your hair
before or after you comb it

Yeah, you just take your electric razor
and start shaving your face in the morning
but keep on going
up over and around your head
and you're done
No regrets

Smooth Clean Bald
Just bald— with no regrets

## ON READING AND WRITING

I've been reading a lot lately
more than I ever have before
but I do now have the luxury
of having more time to do so—
Retirement

Morning is my best time for reading
My best time for concentrating
My best time for writing

I haven't kept count
but I know I am reading
at least two books a month
probably more
Mostly history and biography

In my twenties
I read a lot of Kurt Vonnegut
Many people of my generation
at that age read Vonnegut
and probably went *On the Road*
with Jack Kerouac too

I think of the Vonnegut books—
I first read *Slaughterhouse Five*
and I have re-read it at different points in my life
and it's actually one of the few books
that Hollywood did a decent job
of adapting to film

Hollywood usually does a mediocre job
of adapting books to film
Too many cooks in the kitchen
I suspect is what spoils the soup

If you're too lazy to read
and use the age-old excuse:
    *I'll wait for the movie*
Big mistake—

because in almost all cases
the movie pales compared to the book
Too many changes
Too much added drama
Keep in mind the term "based upon"

Even the Hollywood attempts to portray history
are "based upon"
and could classify as "fiction based on fact"

Another of the few decent attempts
to stay true to the story
was the first film adaptation of the book *Carrie*
by Stephen King

In my twenties
I also read a lot of Stephen King
I was reading more fiction and novels then

I think maybe my high school
and college days were too near past
and that history and biography were learning
and learning seemed too much like high school
but now I am the complete opposite:
I generally only read if I'm learning—
I can't get enough of it

Reading
and neatly underlining passages
with pencil and a straight edge
as a future reference—
to glance at later
Sort of making an abridged edition
within the book

As a twenty-something
Stephen King
was someone I read a lot of
beginning with *Carrie*
then *Salem's Lot*
then *The Shining*

I recall when I read *The Shining*
I was twenty or twenty-one
working in a factory
in the suburbs of Detroit
in an industrial area along I-75
for $3.90 an hour

I would read the book on weekdays
when the line was down for repairs
or as it was being set up for another job run
and even during the day
with all those people and the noise around me
I would occasionally look over my shoulder
startled
King's narrative was that spooky to me

Charley Mobley knew I was reading the book
and one time
when I dragged a barrel of vinyl scraps
over to dump it in the scrap bin
I tipped the barrel up to dump it
and Charley sprang up
from under the pile of vinyl scraps in the bin
and scared the living daylights out of me

One time the line was down for repairs
and I was reading
sometimes glancing to my right
and seeing a shower of sparks
where Benny was working
maybe fifty feet down the line from me—
I continued to read
and glanced down there, now and then
at the shower of sparks

Benny got a higher rate of pay
when he was doing maintenance on the line
maybe fifty or sixty-five cents more per hour

A few pages went by, and I thought to myself
    *What the hell is he up to down there?*

So, I closed the book on a finger
to keep my place
and strolled down the line towards Benny
and his shower of sparks

Benny was grinding away
on the end of a shaft on a roller
that had nothing to do with repairing anything

As a new shower of sparks
shot into the air I half shouted
so he could hear me over the grinder
        *Hey, Benny! What are ya doin'?*
He shouted back *I'm makin' sparks!*
        *What?* I said and started laughing
Benny took his finger off the trigger
and the grinder slowed to a halt
*I'm makin' sparks* he said again
and with that
he started another shower of sparks

I walked back to my station on the line
and as Benny finished up his "repair"
I read a few more pages
about the strange happenings in the hallways
rooms, and on the grounds
of the snowbound Overlook Hotel

I bought and read *The Stand* in Hollywood
when it first came out in 1978
and read it again in the early Eighties
when I lived in San Francisco

The irony is that both times I read this story
about a worldwide pandemic
I caught a cold shortly after starting it
Yeah— Captain Trips—
I was a bit concerned—
Tom Cullen, in the book, would have said:
    "M-O-O-N
    *that spells* concerned"

Of his first twelve novels
I read all but two of them
and it was the twelfth one called *IT*
where he lost me
*IT* was an eleven-hundred-page behemoth
and by page 700 I was thinking:
>        *This better be worth it*
>        *after I've invested this much of my time*

My brother Rick had bought it too
and we were both reading it at the same time
He got ahead of me and said after he was finished
>        *Don't bother*
>        *Save the time it would take*
>        *to read the last four hundred pages*
>        *and read another book*

I put it down
never finished it and moved on
and the only Stephen King I've read since then
was the book *Misery*

My Dad kept reading King
and he sent me two he had read back then
I put them on the shelf and never read them

I pulled them off the shelf last night
and blew the dust off of them
*Rose Madder* and *Bag o' Bones*
In Dad's handwriting is written
*1997* in one and *1998* in the other
They've been sitting on the shelf all that time
Sorry, Dad
I can't remember if I even thanked you for them
I promise to read them someday

So— Yeah—
Anyway—
I picked up another King book a few days back
called *On Writing*
and I'm enjoying it

Even if you don't write anything
you might enjoy reading about how he does it
and why

Done in the classic Stephen King style
where he'll give you
an example of a bad sentence
and follow it with:
     *"Man, who farted, right?"*
Lessons from the Master!

And why am I reading it?
Well, because I'm interested
Do I think I'll ever write a novel?
I don't think so
I used to think I had some ideas
but I think I'm pretty much OK
with just rambling on
in these long-winded poems of mine
if that's what you want to call them—
Poems?
Are they?
I'm not even sure anymore—
They look like poems
I think
Maybe—
but—
Man, who farted, right?

I mean—
I get where he's coming from with that—
I recall once wanting to experience old Westerns
and I asked my Dad for his advice
and he said to pick up a Zane Grey
Then I picked up a Brand...
Brand... Brand... Brand
Max...
Max Brand I think his name was
Then I found one by someone
whose name I don't recall
that was absolutely awful

The author's attempt at what he thought
was actual dialog in authentic accents
was just pathetic
Page after page of flatulence
So—
yeah—
I had to open all the windows in the apartment
to air things out after that one
Whew!
I don't wish a whiff of that one
on any *dadgum dern polecat*

So—
I brought my car in for some service yesterday
and I'm sitting in the waiting room
only me
reading the King book
and one of the Service Department guys
walks by me and says
>       *Wow! It's really nice*
>       *to see someone reading a book*
>       *instead of playing with a phone*
and sadly—
yeah—
it's becoming a rare thing
to see someone reading a book

Maybe phones should fart—
I mean— not all the time
but maybe at a predetermined time limit
the phone could start emitting an odious bouquet
while people look around the waiting room
or office saying
>       *Don't look at me*
>       *It's not my phone*

But they'd have to do something
like walk outside
or stick it in their pocket or purse
because as long as they kept playing with it
it would just keep stinking

124

and if they don't stop—
the phone could ratchet it up
by sounding audible farts
that would keep getting louder and louder
and couldn't be muted

I mean—
maybe people
would get their faces out of their phones
and pay attention to their surroundings
and the people around them
maybe read a book
maybe even put the phone away
and talk to someone
    and say
        *Man, who farted, right?*

# THESE ARE DIFFERENT TIMES

While reading a book
about Walt Whitman this morning
I was struck by quoted words of his
That he would take a ferry
from Brooklyn to Manhattan and back
    *"To get... the pure air*
    *at the economical price of a penny a trip."*

To be out on the East River
between the two cities
where the air may be fresher for that brief period
at a penny a trip

We, in this day and age, tend to forget
or may have never thought about
what cities were like before flush toilets
before sanitation systems

Cities were not only the hub
of commerce and finance
they were also a center of stink
filth and disease

And not only
was there the question of human waste—
These were the days before cars
when the horse
was the quickest means of transportation
and could haul the heavy loads

So, aside from the human waste problem
there was the problem of city streets
with tons of manure and horse urine on them

It's no wonder
that someone might spend a penny
to take a ferry ride
out into the middle of the East River
    to get at *the pure air*

I also recall reading
a book of Norman Rockwell
who wrote about paying a call
on an old gentleman he employed
as a model for his paintings

This was in the days before the telephone
when "calling" someone meant paying a visit
It meant going to the place they lived
their residence

You made a call—
a visit to see if they were home
and if they weren't
you left them your "calling card"
(if you could afford to have them made)
perhaps with a note
to show them you had been there

This was at a time
before elevators in apartment buildings
and Rockwell walked up six flights of stairs
in the dark
to reach the old gent's apartment

The old gent was not at home
but the door must have been unlocked
as Rockwell described what it was like
to be six stories above New York City
How much quieter it was
How much cooler
and how much fresher the air smelled
as he looked out the window at the view
and left a note along with his calling card

And I leave this literary calling card
that someone may or may not ever read
just to remind us of a few of the things
we may no longer think about

These are different times

## THE BEST THING
### (To JMcS)

The best thing
　　about you and me
　　　　is that we are we

# A WEDDING POEM

Love is a glance
   an embrace
      a mingling of emotions
Love is a search for a soulmate
   to share and cherish
      each passing moment

This passing moment is a prelude
   This very day
      is a celebration of trust
        of understanding

This passing moment is a promise
   An awakening
      A sun rising on a new era
        A new tomorrow

This passing moment
   is ours to share
      to savor
   and to hold in our hearts
forever

## DEATH AND TAXES

It has been said
that only two things in life are certain:
Death and taxes
But I think they're forgetting a third—
Farts are funny

Ask any ten-year-old
and I think an answer to the affirmative
will be unanimous

Fizzers and squeakers
and squealers and whooshers
and those that just go *BLAAAAT!*

Farts are funny

It's just one of the laws of Nature
You know it
I know it
but it's one of those things
that are never discussed
in a school science course
or any book of philosophy

And so—
let it be said
that only three things in Life are certain:
Death—
Taxes—
and farts are funny

Fizzzzzzzzzzz
   squeak
     *BLAAAAT!*

## LIFE ON MIDNIGHT SHIFT

A state of constant fatigue
with moments of wakefulness and alertness
but
it seems
only moments

Out of balance
Out of sorts
Not sure when to sleep
or what to eat
or when and where

If you start an activity
are you going to finish it?

All seems temporary
and never quite the same
or maybe it's exactly the same
but completely different

Thoughts pause—
go blank—
missing—
and come back with the shake of the head—

maybe

## GOOD TIMES, GREAT ADVENTURE

Midnight shift
One hour of sleep in the past thirty
and here I am in Yosemite Valley again
in a simple
small
one room cabin in Camp Curry
Two by four frame and panel
two beds
desk and chair
one shelf
all well-worn

Surrounded by the majestic walls of granite
I walk this valley floor
in awe of the splendor
the wonder
the wildness of it all
on such a mighty, massive scale

This evening, we rest
Tomorrow, we rise early
eat
and head on out and up
to the Porcupine Creek trailhead
on the Tioga Road to the north
and then a six-and-a-half-mile hike
to the top of Yosemite Falls—
just to say we did it

And we did it—
my son Frank and I
with views of Half Dome
North Dome
Cloud's Rest
The Clark Range
Glacier Point
Cathedral Peaks
All of it
All of it for miles

Miles and miles and miles around us
Phenomenal
as far as you could see
Horizon to horizon

Lost the trail for a bit
as we observed a boulder-sized chunk
of pure white quartz
dropped by a glacier so long ago
carried here from who knows where

Near there
a doe came so close to us
that we could hear her breathe
The peace
The solitude
No sounds but the wind
the water
birds
and our boots on the trail

And as the boots hit the trail on the way back
a ligament in my left knee was shouting:
    *Hey! You up there!*
    *I've had enough for today!*
and muscles near the bottoms of both thighs
were cramping painfully and shouting:
    *Us too! Knock it off, ya clown!*
    *How young do you think you are?*
And I passed along a message to them all
in a quiet understanding way
*Listen guys*, I said
*I know you're all 52 years-old*
*and you certainly have a right to complain*
*but my heart and spirit are 22 today*
*So—*
*bear with me on this*
*There's only one way out*
*and there's about six and a half more miles to go*
*and much of it uphill*

The knee and thighs grumbled back:
*Well, we don't have to like it*
*and nothing says we have to allow you*
*to enjoy it either, buddy!*

And, believe me, they didn't allow me to enjoy
those last six and a half miles
Grumbling and stabbing me with pains
Pains that I had not known on younger hikes
I'm getting older
but I'm not allowing that to stand in my way

We made it back to the truck
Frank before me
and I'll be the first to admit
that on the last uphill stretch
I could only take about five steps
before stopping
panting
resting
But I got there
we got there
exhausted
but we got there

Back in the valley
we took well-deserved showers
ate
and laid down for a much-needed rest
sleeping in the little cabin
with all the windows open
on a still, dark night
We both went out like a light

The next day was also beautiful
Drenched in sunshine
Pure— dazzling—
We wandered the valley
looking for a nice spot with a view
to snack on a lunch
before heading back to civilization

A must
A little tradition
started by my old trail partner Eric and I:
Find a great view
sit down and break bread one last time
before traveling back to the routine
the mundane
the same old same old

So, we found a large fallen log out in a meadow
with a splendid view of Yosemite Falls
and sat with our backs against the log
snacking on small items
drinking water
and gazing up to where we were standing
at the top of the falls
just the day before

Good times— Great adventure
   This is what life is for!
      Enjoy!

## DON'T QUIT YOUR DAY JOB

If you think you have writer's block
and can't think of anything to write about
to explore
    to comment on
        to satirize
reach into your pocket
pull out a few coins
and go buy a newspaper
scan through it
and if you still think
you have nothing to write about
then go find something else to do
and whatever you do—

don't quit your day job

## WE HAVE THE POWER

We have been living in an era
of corporate and political overreach
that has lasted roughly fifty to sixty years
An era of deregulation
hostile takeovers
magnificent greed
Whole communities decimated with factory closings
by corporations that turned their backs
on the American Working Class
who made them the mighty corporations they are
in the first place

Is it merely economic erosion?
Or is it a deliberate campaign to destabilize
decimate and destroy
one of America's greatest contributions
to humankind?—
    (The Middle Class)

A strong Middle Class
with purpose and pride
durability and dignity
and the world's highest standard of living
for the Working Class majority

The Working Class were once desperately poor
despite working 14-hours a day
6 days a week
Living in company dorms and housing
with their children ill-fed
ill-clothed
ill-educated
and perhaps working alongside their parents
for pennies
when they should have been bringing an apple
to their teacher at school

The same Working Class in America
that fought for generations

to make child labor illegal
Fought to reduce the working day
from 14 or 16 hours a day
down to 12 hours
then to 10
then to 8
and from 6 days a week down to 5 days

Families could now spend time together
as they had not been able to before
Children and adults
both now had the time to educate themselves
to better themselves
and to simply have rest and leisure

One song they sang then had these words:
> *Eight hours for work*
> *Eight hours for rest*
> *Eight hours for what we will*

Was that asking too much?

The Working Class of the 19th century
fought for fair wages
sick leave
holidays
weekends
safer working conditions
pensions
and simply to be paid on time
regularly
with cash
rather than company "scrip"
that could only be exchanged
at the company owned store

And they were met with resistance
for over 100 years
by not only the company
and their "security" goon squads
but by local authorities
judges

militias sent by governors
and sometimes even the White House
but they fought on for fair living conditions

And unfortunately
many times that fighting
was not merely arguing
petitioning or striking
it was actual bloodshed
imprisonment and brutal beatings
men hung from the gallows
or shot dead where they stood
Women and children caught in the crossfire
or burnt to death in fires
set by the militias
It truly was class warfare

But— in time—
sensibility and reason prevailed
and there was an elevation
of the Working Class
as the world had never seen before

Children taken from the mills and factories
who not only learned their ABCs
but went on to the colleges and universities
and became the teachers for the next generation

This was unheard of before
It had never been achieved

This became the Middle Class
who could own property
who had the freedom to assemble
and the freedom to have privacy
The freedom of choice and to use their voice
The freedom to vote for candidates
who would represent them
The freedom to vote
for ideas to become laws
promoting fairness for all

The freedom to organize Unions
for the workplace
and it was that voice and that vote
that was the power of the Working Class

We have the power to do more than make a living—
we have the power to make a difference

A positive difference
A peaceful difference
A sensible and reasonable difference

Let us not sleepwalk through history
as the tide is turned against us
Let us not stand silently and scatter

There is no politician
who cannot be barred from office
by the Working Class of America
and there is no politician
who cannot be removed from office
by the Working Class of America

We have the power—
    We simply must vote!

We have the power to make change possible
    Peaceably

We have the power to turn the tide of history

We have the power to reverse this overreach
that has unfairly targeted the Working Class

We have the power to make this world
a just and fair place for all

We—
    The Working Class
        We have the power!

## PULLING MY LEG

I remember somebody telling me once
when I was a child—
my Mom or Dad
or maybe a Grandparent—
Anyway—
somebody told me
that if you swallow a watermelon seed
it will start to grow in your belly

Come to think of it—
that sounds like something
my Grampa Frank would say
He had a mischievous side to him
and he liked to freak us kids out
by pushing his dentures
part way out of his mouth
with his tongue
and then retracting them
First the upper plate
then the lower one
then lean back with a smile
and his big belly-shaking laugh

Anyway—
with the watermelon seeds
my child-like imagination
started turning the little gears upstairs
and I began to envision sprouts and leaves
slowly appearing from my nose and ears
and I began to worry

Grampa Frank had an artificial leg
Flesh-colored aluminum
as I recall—
His one leg was taken off
from just below the knee down
in a coal mining accident
from his younger years

Apparently
the men worked in pairs down in the mine
and his partner hadn't warned him
about a coal car coming down the tracks
It knocked Grampa over
and severed his leg just below the knee
and he never saw that partner guy again
He either left town out of guilt
or a fear that Grampa Frank
would thrash him a good one someday

Grampa Frank had some wild times

I sat up drinking beers with him
one night when I was twenty
(which is a whole other story for another time)
and he showed me a knuckle
on one of his big hands
that looked divided by a crack
           *See that?* he said
           *That was a guy down in Texas*
           *when I was in the Army*
He looked down at his knuckle and said
           *Almost killed him*

I guess in his younger years
he could lose himself in a bottle
and had some fight inside of him
My Mom told me of a time when she was a kid
and he brawled out in the kitchen of the house
with some guy for some reason

But we kids knew him
after those days had played themselves out
and he had mellowed down
into a big-bellied Grampa
who would sit in his chair
for his morning coffee
out in the living room
of their little three-room cabin
on a river in Pennsylvania

stripped to the waist
only his pants on
and every morning he would let go
with one tremendous sneeze
I've never heard one louder!
You'd see it coming on his face and
BOOM!!!
He'd let it go
and wherever the cat was laying on the floor
it would spring up
a good twelve inches into the air
and Grampa Frank would have a good, long laugh

Anyway—
He had this flesh-colored aluminum leg
and I recall him sitting on the back porch
up at my Folk's cabin on Lake Michigan
tapping it with a screwdriver
absentmindedly
        *tink-tink-tink*
and a neighbor boy named Mickey
who was about five or six at the time
listened and looked
        *tink-tink-tink*
and finally, his curiosity got the best of him
and he asked Grampa
        *Why does your leg sound like that?*
With that leg resting on his good one
Grampa Frank looked at Mickey
lifted up the pant leg and kept tapping
        *You mean this?* he asked
        *Yeah* said Mickey

Now, on each side of the aluminum leg
there was a round ventilation hole
about an inch and a half round
and Grampa kept tapping the leg
        *tink-tink-tink*
and then he stopped—
held the screwdriver over the hole
and let it drop into one hole

and out the other side
all the way through the leg
and down to the porch boards

Mickey's eyes flew open wide
and he backed up a few steps
into the porch railing
as Grampa laughed and said
> *What's the matter?*
> *You never seen a leg like that?*
> *Can't you do that with your leg?*
Mickey remained wide-eyed and silent
crept over to the steps
took off running down them
and kept running across the dune
towards the Kelly's cottage as Grampa laughed
and we kids were shouting
> *Come back, Mickey!*
> *It's not real!!*
but off he ran home
to tell his sisters and brother

Well—
I don't think there's too much
to that watermelon seed story
I never have seen leaves or sprouts
come out of my nose or ears
or belly button
and I'm sure I've eaten
a whole lot more tomato seeds
And corn?
Heck—
corn is nothing but seeds

Nope—
no corn stalks growing out of my butt
No leaves or sprouts

I have a feeling that Grampa Frank
was just pulling my leg

## OVER AT RAY'S

For some reason today
a memory of the ice cream store
in the old neighborhood crossed my mind—
Ray's

The sign simply said:

=RAY'S=
ICE CREAM

And we all called it Ray's in the neighborhood
We'd say:
*Hey, let's go to Ray's*
*See you at Ray's*
*I'm going over to Ray's*

It was a smaller store then
A Mom-and-Pop operation
a block up and over from our house on Edgar Street
past the bowling alley
which most people called
    Bow-LAIR-o
while others pronounced it
    BOW-lee-row
and beyond Ray's there wasn't much of anything
all the way up to 14-Mile Road

At that young age
I recall always getting a sugar cone
with a scoop of "Peppermint Stick" on top
and Boy, Oh Boy! —
it was just like a cold, creamy candy cane
and just what any little boy or girl would want
anytime any day
anyhow any way
and just ten cents got you a scoop, back then
Mom always got the Coffee ice cream
which I later graduated to
once the pure sugar
candy cravings of a kid had passed

Ray was a white-haired man with glasses
in a white shirt and white pants
Everyone behind the counter wore white back then
Dresses for the women
Shirts and pants for the men

A stand-up/walk-up counter to the right
with a cash register
and on the left a long curving counter
of pearly gray Formica
winding its way around
with stools to sit on with round red cushions
A checkerboard of black and white tiles on the floor

When I was a little older, I had a paper route
The Detroit News
A small route
only two streets— Edgar and Coolidge
and a little piece of Starr Road in between

And I'm not sure why
they didn't just give one street each
to the routes on either side of me
but they didn't
So, that's all I had
Just the two blocks

And I liked my little paper route
that is, until one summer
when a kid down the block took over for me
while I was gone up north
and he pulverized the route
When I came back for the school year
there were only about a dozen customers left
He just wiped it out
And at a three-cent commission
that only made for thirty-six cents a day
Hardly worth the effort

But when it was a healthy route
I enjoyed it

Three cents on each daily
Seven cents on each Sunday paper
and on days when the paper was thin
I could put them all in a canvas shoulder bag
and walk my little route
On the days with thicker editions
I'd throw a double bag over the back of my bike

Rain?
Yeah, you still had to do it
Snow?
Yep, get out there
Get it done

The paper station was a few blocks away
almost to the railroad tracks
down a dead-end industrial street
It was a small one-room brick building
with rough tables of plywood and two-by-fours
where we all "stuffed" our papers
with the advertisement sections

Mr. Zarate ran the station
He was always in a good mood
He always called the newspapers "bananas"
You'd call out your route number
and he'd count out your bananas and stack 'em
and you'd move 'em to an empty table
where you could stuff 'em and put 'em in your bags

Sunday mornings were Big Bananas Day
Big thick heavy papers
and always more of them
Every route had more Sunday-only customers
sometimes twice as many
and that was the day you saw some Dads there
sitting in idling cars outside
as their boys stuffed the bananas inside

Dad would wake me up on Sundays at six-o'clock
and he'd fire up his 1962 white Valiant Slant-6

the kind with the three-speed shifter
on the steering column
    *three-on-the-tree*
we called those transmissions

Anyway-
he'd putt along slowly
with the white Valiant in first gear
the trunk lid up
listening to the radio and smoking cigarettes
(he was smoking, not me... yet)
I'd grab the papers from the trunk
and walk them up to the houses
and then we'd go home
and Dad would get another cup of coffee
with the last newspaper
while I crawled back into bed

And then "collection day" came around
which was never any one day in particular
Any weekday after school and before dinner would do
and I'd put my coin changer on my belt
the type with four tubes
one each for quarters, dimes, nickels and pennies
A slot at the top to drop coins in
A lever at the bottom of each tube
to dispense the coins
one coin at a time

Sixty-five cents change would be
click-click on the quarters
a click on the dimes
and a click on the nickels
    *click-e-click*
    *click*
    *click*
    Thank you, Ma'am
and on to the next house I'd go
Ninety cents a week for those who had
both the daily and the Sunday delivered
Thirty-five cents for Sunday only

I'd get the occasional bonehead
who wouldn't pay me for weeks
always sending me away
or not answering the door
Then I'd finally catch them home
and tell them that they owed ten weeks
      *TEN WEEKS?!!* they'd shout at me
Well, yes, sir.
You keep sending me away week after week

They'd disappear from the door
come back thrusting nine dollars at me and shout
      *TEN WEEKS?!!*
      *YOU CAN KEEP YOUR DAMN PAPERS!*
and slam the door in my face
No tip

I never could quite figure out that kind of customer
What-in-the-world did I do to deserve that?
I think that's when I began to question
the average intelligence of the public
in general

But I had my share of good customers
who would tip me
be pleasant and polite
And as for the rude tightwads
who never tipped or were nasty—
Sunday morning was
      *The Paperboy's Revenge*
A good slam on the screen door
early Sunday morning with that big, heavy paper
      ***WHAM!!!***
Especially effective if they had a dog
that barked and went wild
when I smacked the screen door with the paper
      ***WHAM!!!***
*Take that you nasty tightwad—*
*heh-heh-heh-heh*
and I'd walk away
with a mischievous little grin

So, anyway—
once the collecting was done
I'd click sixty-five cents from my coin changer
and head down Coolidge to Ray's
sit at the long curving counter
and order a chocolaty malted milkshake
and share it— with me, myself and I

A little reward for another week's worth
of walking my little Detroit News paper route
and it was a great chocolate malted
A fantastic reward—
And the folks at Ray's all dressed in white
didn't just fill the tall heavy glass— no—
they poured to the top of the glass
and then set the metal mixing cup next to it
with a long-handled spoon
so you could have all that too
and usually, you could pour and scrape
about another half serving out of there
and into your big, heavy milkshake glass

And although I don't miss
the occasional bonehead on that route
and although I'm glad that I make more
than the seven to nine dollars a week
that little route paid—
I do miss those chocolate malted milkshake rewards
Yep— Ray's made the best

And I have never had a chocolate malted
that tasted quite as good
as those milkshakes after collection day
when you'd find me a block up and over
from our little house on Edgar Street
sitting at the long, curving counter
scraping that last of a chocolate malted
out of a metal mixing cup
and licking the last of it
off the long-handled spoon—
    over at Ray's

## IF NOT NOW— WHEN?

As I recall
junior high school dances
were few and far between

For my older brothers
I remember them going every week
and I would ride along in the car
with Mom or Dad as we dropped them off
or when we picked them up
at that late, dark, mysterious hour of nine
(or maybe earlier)
and I wondered what went on in there
All I ever saw were kids milling about outside
waiting for parents to pick them up

When I got my turn
the dances were very few
The program had pretty much disappeared
but I do recall being there for some

The gymnasium was rather dim
(mood lighting, I suppose)
Sawdust on the wooden floors
that we boys loved to slide on
but were scolded for doing so
by the teachers who acted as chaperones

The girls all stayed on one side of the gym
a few feet from the wall— standing around
and the boys stayed on the other side
standing around in small groups
talking and teasing
goofing around

For the girls— of course
it was not proper to ask a boy to dance
They could only stand there
nervously waiting

And most of us 12 and 13-year-old boys
were too nervous, awkward and shy
to be seen walking across that vast open space
that vast, massive open frontier
that was between the two sides
        Yikes!
To have all those eyes in the gym watching
as you walked across that vast expanse
        *Who do you think he's going to ask?*
        *What do you think she'll say?*
        *What if she says 'No'?*

Very few danced—
but we all should have been dancing
every one of us should have been dancing
out on that gymnasium floor
young, fresh and free
dancing in one big group
celebrating the youth
that we were all too inexperienced
to realize we had

I recall a band called Jade Angel
that played an excellent version of the Cream song
        *Sunshine of Your Love*
I liked to listen and watch them play
I was too shy for the girls and the dancing
but the rock 'n' roll moved me
and to this day when I hear
        *Sunshine of Your Love*
I am transported back to that gym
with the dim lights
and sawdust on the floor
Jade Angel on the stage

Ah, yes—
we all should have been dancing
in one gigantic, joyous, pulsing group
celebrating youth
celebrating life
young, fresh and free

Each generation knows
they should have done things a little differently

Each generation knows
the awkwardness of the Boy/Girl thing
at first—
and later

Each generation knows they held back
Let opportunities slip through their fingers
        *Maybe she would have said Yes*
Held back feelings of joy felt inside
when they should have been dancing
        *Yeah— maybe she would have said Yes*

Each generation has left hearts broken
by leaving deeds undone
by leaving words unspoken

But each generation also knows
    that it's never too late
        to cross that vast expanse
            and try to live again

And I took a chance— years later
and crossed that vast expanse
of time and distance
to find one of the girls who was at those dances
and do things differently

To not think to myself *What if?*
but to think *If not now— when?*

This time I did ask
And she did say *Yes*

And we are partners now
dancing this Dance of Life
to this very day

If not now—when?

## NOW IS ALWAYS NEW

New beginnings
New ideas
New reasons to revisit old beginnings
and dust off old ideas
old thoughts

Just get out there and do it!

A new year begins
    every morning you rise

Time is linear—
a straight line from Point A to Point B
and every new moment begins *now*
fresh
and will never repeat itself
will never be seen again

Time is now
  and now—
    is always new

# Selected Poems

## From

## Stunning Jagged Edges of Precise Malfunction (2005)

*As the game continues
you should seek to say
ever more clearly
what you truly believe*
-Charles Bukowski

## CROSSROADS

Where life ceases to be solely born
of anguish and oppression
and springs forth a source of understandings
pure and genuine:
this is the crossroads of a civilization

And we stand at the crossroads
  of those feelings

We stand at the crossroads
  of this civilization

It is we in the Present
  we of this very moment
    who must decide
      what will be for our children

It is for them
  and primarily for them
    that we should make these decisions

It is for them
  and us
    and all that surrounds us
      that we should live this very moment
    this sparkle in the sand
  this feeling from within
Peace
  peace
    flowing from within

I shall never tire of life
  or the challenges it provides me

May a drop of wisdom
  touch my forehead
    May it saturate deep within
      and may it penetrate—
        my soul

## A SLOW DRIP

We seem to react to oppression
as if it were a slow drip

                            dropping

from the end    of the faucet
              and    into an empty cup
A slow drip

                        drip

    drip

                    dripping—

There    is nothing threatening
about a slow    drip

        except—

                    that it continues

Society sees it drop
    from the end of the    faucet
        and vanish into    the cup

            there
                    gone

    there  ♦

        gone


   Out of sight

        Out of mind
    Until—  ♦
     the cup fills
 and the surface begins to rise above the rim


      ♦

Each drop threatening the invisible
     fragile boundary
  that holds the water ♦ above the rim



      ♦

  And now that the boundary is threatened
   each drop is full of anxiety
 each drop is brimming with tension
      ♦

    stress
   uneasiness
    disquiet  ♦ concern
         anticipation
         suspense
      ♦

And
 any moment now—
      ♦


      this thing


      ♦


  is going to  overflow


      ♦


      ♦


      ♦

## THE KISS

Remember your very first kiss?
I do

Call me sentimental
call me corny
call me a sap
but I do remember my very first kiss
and I remember the date
many, many years ago tonight
many, many years after The Kiss
I write this

Many, many years ago
and I still remember The Kiss
     the girl
        the street
           the magic

That soft
       warm
            electrifying kiss

The kiss that opened a new era
a new chapter in The Book of Life
The kiss that whispered:
     *Your childhood is over*
*and all time will now be known as*
          *Before The Kiss*
              *and*
          *After The Kiss*

It was unexpected
It was exciting
It was inspiring

It was a hot summer night
after a ballgame at Memorial Park
walking her home in the humid heat
of a short Midwestern summer

Can't remember the teams
Don't recall the score—
Who cares?
The game wasn't the point anyway

Being close and being together was
Sensing something new
Experiencing something new
Feeling something new

That was the point of all those hot
humid
short
Midwestern summers

and The Kiss?
    ahhhhh... yes...
        The Kiss

We were walking along the sidewalk
lit only by streetlamps and headlights
and on the corner
she stopped and turned
and softly said—
with a somewhat anxious look
in her soft, glowing eyes
  *Kiss me*
    *Kiss me, Jack*
and closed her eyes

I also closed mine—
  and a new era opened

Always to be remembered
  never to be forgotten
    it was—
      The Kiss

# ONE POINT EIGHT

The other night I saw a show
where a nationally known comedian
was being interviewed
by another nationally known comedian

The guest was making light
of global warming issues
and making the issues sound childishly stupid
by saying things like:
> *One point eight degrees?!*
> *C'mon!*
> *Who can feel*
> *a one point eight-degree difference?*
> *Pah-leeeze!*

A smirk
A laugh
And with a wave of a hand, he continued
> *And twenty years from now*
> *it's to double to three point six degrees?*
> *Whoa!*
> *Yeah— right!*
> *I think my kids can handle that!*

The point is not whether *you* can feel
a one point eight-degree difference
This is *global* warming
You have to think *globally*

Maybe you can't feel the difference
between seventy
and seventy-one point eight degrees
but what about the polar ice caps
and all the world's glaciers?
They will certainly feel the difference
between thirty-one
and thirty-two point eight degrees
The difference between frozen and thawing
which will translate into greater spring runoffs
more flooding and a gradual rise in sea levels

All coastlines would gradually change
All coastal cities
that are now a few feet above sea level
would become what?
Even inland cities along rivers
inland lakes and valleys would be affected

And your children?
Three point six degrees?
They can handle it?
Yeah— maybe *they* can
but now you're talking about
the difference between thirty-one
and thirty-four point six degrees
More flooding and higher sea levels

Sometimes
    what appears to be trivial
        isn't trivial at all

Sometimes small things
    can make a very big difference

Sometimes the difference between
    more-of-the-same
        and instability—
            is one point eight

# KNOTS

My life feels—
  all tied up in knots tonight
    And for every knot I untie
  it seems that debt and circumstance
tie up and tighten twelve more
  to curse at
    and try to untie

I put bait on my line
  throw it in and get a nibble
    (now and then)

But it seems that every time
  I haul in my line
    the bait has disappeared
    and there are twelve more knots
  for me to curse at
and try to untie

When will it end?
  Does it ever end?

I pick at these knots with my fingernails
  I chew at these knots with my teeth
    and sometimes in frustration
  I throw the line down
and walk away

But that doesn't help—
  The knots are still there
    when I pick the line up again
  and always will be
unless I try to untie them

But don't pull the line too tight
  or you'll never get them undone

And don't look to someone else
  to untie your knots

They have knots of their own
  and besides
    why should they untie your knots
    when it's you who put them there
in the first place?

But—
  sometimes your patience breaks
    like a dam on a river
      and there you are—
    trying to deal with a dilemma
  with only a thimble in your hand
trying to divert a raging torrent
  one thimbleful at a time

And sometimes your enthusiasm
  feels like the sails of a ship
    on a dead calm sea—
      slack
    Waiting for the winds
  to carry you away
and try as you may
  you're going nowhere
    until those winds return

And— here I am
  waiting for the wind
    with a thimble in my hand
    trying to untie the knots
of debt and circumstance

I feel all tied up in knots tonight

All tied up in knots

# JULIUS
### (In Memory of Julius Fantucci, Sr.)

The first thing I think of
and the first thing I see
when I think about Julius
is his smile

A big, radiant smile

A smile that lit up the room
or made a sunny day even brighter
and that smile
was always at the ready for you

Julius knew me before I knew him
and I knew him my entire childhood
He was my next door neighbor
The Dad who lived next door

A truck driving family man
who only had to walk a block to work
all those thirty-eight years he drove trucks

I remember him walking to work
in his dark green work clothes
with a lunch pail swinging at his side

I recall because our walk to grade school
was along those same streets
   Edgar to Normandy
   Normandy to Coolidge
and then we kids went on our way
from there to Mandalay

Whenever we saw
a big dark green semi-truck
coming down the street
on our way to or from school
we'd look up into the truck cab
to see if it was Julius behind the wheel

166

and if he was
we'd jump and shout
pumping our left arms up and down
above our heads
and Julius would reach up and pull the cord
which would give a few blasts on the air horn

HAA—WooAAAAH!!!
  HAW!!!
   WooAAAHHHH!!!!

He'd do it several times
with his big smile and a laugh
as we neighborhood kids jumped up and down
hooting and hollering
shouting
  *YEAH!!*
   *WOO-HOO!!*
    *ALRIGHT!!*
and Julius would wave as he drove on
We'd wave back smiling and laughing
as we went on our way to line up
sit down
stand up
face the flag
say our Pledge of Allegiance
and learn to write our cursive loop-dee-loops
on large double-lined paper
or read about the world
from our Weekly Readers
or *Show and Tell* something of interest
jump rope at recess
and see pictures of exotic places
like Japan, England and Oklahoma

One summer
I recall Julius driving us kids
through the cherry orchards up north
in an old black Ford sedan
on a two-rut farm road
with the branches of the trees

heavy with fruit
hanging down on both sides
nearly rendering the road invisible

As he drove on
we put our hands out the rolled down windows
grabbing handfuls of red tart cherries
and stuffing them into our mouths
laughing and jerking back
as the branches seemed to reach in
and try to pull us out of the car
and into the orchard

When you grow up next door to someone
your entire childhood
they become like family to you
Second parents
Like a second Mom and Dad
or an Aunt and Uncle you were very close to

I recall leaving home for my final time
I was twenty-two
and knew in my bones
that it was the last night
I'd ever live in my parents' home

Of those I felt I needed
to say *See ya later* to
Irene and Julius came to mind

It was twilight in early September
when I drifted over next door
and there was Julius
sitting on his front porch steps
a smile and a hello as usual
and he slapped the front porch and said
  *One more payment, Jack*
  *One more payment and it's mine*
He was happy
He was contented
He was Julius

And I recall whenever he was up north
at my Folks' log cabin
that he'd be down in the lake
first thing every morning
and we kids thought he was nuts!

But now—
I myself do the same thing
anytime I'm camping out behind the cabin
Out of the tent and into the lake
first thing in the morning
Hoooo – Weeee!!!
What a wake-up call!
No wonder he did that!

There was a time
when eighteen years had passed
since I had seen the old neighborhood
That's a lot of space
That's a lot of time
and I wasn't even sure I'd do it then

It was a last-minute decision
but I decided to go
to my 30th high school reunion

I dropped in on the old neighborhood
that hot August afternoon
The huge old Elm trees
shading the street and front yards

And I stopped in to say hello
to Irene and Julius
Eighty-two and eighty-one
bless their hearts
We sat at their kitchen table
eating meat loaf and corn bread
and chatted and laughed

Then I went down the street
and sat on the porch with Bob Cleghorn

another neighborhood Dad who knew me
before I knew him
and I'm so glad I did

Julius passed on just a few months later
and I could say that I'll miss seeing
that big smile of his
but I won't miss it
because I still see it
and I always will

Julius—
thanks for the smiles
and all the blasts from the air horn
thanks for taking us kids to ball games
and for letting us kids
get our hands and mouths drenched
with fresh, tart cherry juice
in that childhood orchard of long ago

Yes, the first thing I think of
and the first thing I see
when I think about Julius
is his smile

And I've been trying to find
some other way to say this
because it's not an easy thing to do

It's not an easy thing to say—
but—

So long, Julius
So long, Second Dad
Old friend
Pal

So long—
and keep smiling

## EMBRACING SHADOWS

My purpose in life
  has blown away with the wind
    never to return—
      (but it will)

The wind circles around and around
  The tide goes out
    and comes in again
The snow falls from the clouds
  melts on the mountains
    and returns to the clouds once more

Sometimes it feels
  like trying to make ends meet
    while the ends keep moving
      farther and farther apart

Or like trying to carry water
  uphill
    with a sieve

Or like trying to make a sculpture
  from air

Or trying to embrace a shadow

And I've been embracing shadows
  and sculpting air
    for quite some time now

And I'll be embracing shadows
  and sculpting air
    for some time to come

There is frustration
  and satisfaction in knowing—
    it is what I do best

# MY FRONT PAGE

Surely
there must be something good to report
something good to write about
There must be

I know that my own world
(the one I walk around in)
is not represented
on the front page of the daily news

Take
for example
the front page of the day I write this poem:
Foreign president assassinated
Election fraud in the Philippines
Genocide in Africa
Murder
Rape
Gas prices jump
Does the news always have to be like this?

Surely
there was something good that happened today
Surely
there could be a balance of bad and good
Surely
it could be at least fifty-fifty

Maybe they could split it up into sections
and all the bad news
could go into the Bad Section—
your daily dose
of depression and disorder
destruction and dysfunction
social decay

Why do the newspapers and broadcasters
feel they must focus on only the worst
that Humanity has to offer?

I mean—
for a moment—
make your own front page
Think about it
Ponder it

Here's my front page:
in big, bold black letters
the main headline would shout:

## HE WOKE UP!

Isn't that good enough news
in and of itself?
To wake up
and experience another day of this miracle
this cosmic coincidence called Life
and then— read on
The next headline in smaller print:

### HE WORKED AN OVERTIME SUNDAY SHIFT

Hey, a boost to my economy
There's some good news

Read further into the story
and it will say:
### He left his shift
### with the same amount of fingers
### he came in with
More good news

And another small headline
### HE ATE
No famine in my world today
no rape
no murder
I assaulted no one
I swindled no one
There's plenty of good news
in our own little worlds

I can't believe that the world is as bad
as the news makes it out to be

It's like the coverage
of the 1989 earthquake in San Francisco
when you were only shown
one block of burning buildings
up in the Marina District
over and over again
which gave the world the impression
that the whole city was burning down

I was getting phone calls from back east:
  *Are you OK?*
  *What a tragedy!*
  *Your whole city is burning down!*
  *How about your place?*
I'd say: *Relax—*
*In the whole city there's only a block or two burning*
*I'm OK*

But I get the feeling
that we think the whole world's on fire
when it's only a small part of it

I mean to say—
Most of us are good
Most of us do right
Whatever the country
whatever the culture
most people are good
and only desire good things for themselves
their children and family
their friends and neighbors

Surely
there must be something good to report
something good to write about
There must be

And there you have it—
Today's news from my point of view
My front page
What's on yours?

# EVER-CHANGING

If only these feelings could linger
  interweave
    and entwine themselves
  within the fibers
of our everyday lives!

If these moments
  these gems in the sunlight
    could somehow linger with us
as we jump
  from boulder to boulder
    in our day-to-day existence

We jump—
        from boulder
  to
      boulder
          to

    boulder

and experience what we must
  what we shall
    and at times— what we wish

It is a river of Time
  that we meander down

A river of subtle moments
  Of white-water rapids
    Of slippery, loose rocks and log jams
      but— somehow we do it

Somehow we do it—
  as the clouds pass overhead
  entwining and mingling
    lingering—

    ever-changing

# ALL IS ONE

During my brief young college days
I remember a whole host of ideas
wandering around on campus

Those into Yoga or Buddhism
or Eastern Spiritualism
or socialism
this-ism, that-ism
or any kind of ism
that was currently the cool-ism
The Ism-of-the-Month

Environmentalists
Left-wing government-haters
Right-wing government-hater haters
Bible-toting in-your-face young Christians
born-again or dyed-in-the-wool from birth

A whole host of ideas wandered around
on those mildly warm
sunny autumn afternoons
up in northern Michigan

I remember a group of guys with goofy grins
and a dreamy look in their eyes
who would wander around on campus
and walk up to you and say: *All is One*

And I would ask
  *What is One?*

        and they would say
        *One is everything*

And I would ask
  *What is everything?*

        and they would say
        *Everything is Universal*

And I would ask
*What is Universal?*

    and they would say
    *All is Universal*

And I would ask
*Well, what is All?*

    and they would say
    *All is One*
        and wander away with goofy grins

I laid back on the grass
alone
with my hands behind my head
gazing up through the leaves and branches
at flashes of blue sky and dazzling sunlight
and thought to myself
    *All is One*
and smiled

An interesting idea: *All is One*

But— *what*— is One?
I mean—
the "All" part is pretty straightforward
but what about this "One" stuff?
If All is One
then what is the common thread
that binds it all together?

Art

*ART?!!!* you say
*How could Art be the common thread*
*of everything known to us?*
*Known to us and our five senses*
*touch smell taste sight hearing*
*Known to us and our other sense*
*which is the emotion we feel within*

It all depends on your definition of Art

Nature has sometimes been hailed
throughout the Ages
as the highest of the Arts
and it is the highest Art
It is the only Art
It is the Living Art
It creates itself
and all that lies within it

Somewhere thousands of years ago
a group of early scholars
decided that there were seven Arts
and they cleverly called them:
      The Seven Arts

And those Seven Arts are:
Music
Dance
Novel
Drama
Sculpture
Painting
and Architecture— yes, Architecture
(the all-but-forgotten runt-of-the-litter)

But I feel there is only one Major Art:
Nature— the Living Art
And that within that one Major Art
lies those seven categories
or The Seven Arts
and within those Seven Arts
you will find everything known to us

There are common forms
of each of the Seven Arts
and refined forms of each
and the key is in the common forms

In common terms:

Music is the Art of Sound
Dance is the Art of Motion
Novel is the Art of Writing
Drama is bringing a Writing to life
Sculpture is the Art of Form
Painting is the Art of Color and Light
and Architecture is a practical form of Sculpture

Now—
think of a conversation you may have had today
How many of the Seven Arts
were involved in your conversation?

The Art of Music certainly was
if you can speak and hear
and if you cannot
the Art of Motion replaced Music
as hand and facial gestures
conveyed the message

In either case
common forms of Art were used:
sound and motion
And, if spoken
the conversation could've been written out
as Music on paper
since both voices had tempo and pitch
and moved along with a rhythm of syllables
and pauses—
of—
silence

You were indeed speaking in tones
and rhythms
and rests—
of—
silence
You were using a common form of Music

And what were you doing with those tones—
that Music?

Exchanging information or ideas?
Telling a story of some sort?
Fiction or factual
premeditated or improvisational
and doing so in perhaps a dramatic way
with zest and enthusiasm
or grief and sadness
with concern and alertness
with comedy or tragedy

Perhaps your hands and arms
perhaps your whole body was in motion
punctuating your words and ideas as you spoke

Music Novel Drama Dance

Perhaps you were sitting on a chair
at a table in a café

Sculpture and Architecture

And perhaps the chair, table and café
were painted in a common way

Music Novel Drama Dance
Sculpture Painting and Architecture
in very basic and common forms
but all seven were present

Your conversation won't make the charts
won't be a hit— but it was Music

Take a walk in the woods on a breezy summer day
listen to the wind
moving briskly through the trees
rustling leaves
and whispering softly through pine needles
Music Motion Nature Peace
You are walking through Living Art
Trees are living Sculpture
that Nature creates and maintains

Take a walk along a shore of glistening white sand
Experience the Music and Motion
of waves tumbling over themselves
crashing
reaching to the beach
and sliding back to crash again
and again
and again
in perpetual motion
Listen to the birds singing overhead
and among the trees in the forest behind you
Music and Motion
Living Art

And you yourselves are Living Art
A marvelous example of Sculpture
Living Sculpture
You are Living Art

To me—
Art is not merely a pastime
diversion or entertainment
It is Life
And being an Artist
is not merely a hobby or a career
It is a way of Life— a belief
a belief that I am comfortable with

Art lives and breathes and changes as we all do
Its realm is the Universe
the cosmos and beyond
The Grand Canyon
The Rocky Mountains
The Sierra Nevada Range
Any wilderness you walk into

And we are all Artists—
Some in basic ways
Others in more practiced ways
And I try to practice my beliefs daily
I try to live and breathe them

Whatever you believe is within you—
in your world—
and you must be at peace with yourself

Believe in what you wish
Carry it with you
Be comfortable with it
Practice it

As long as it does not harm you
or harm others
you must be on the right path

Believe in yourself—

Believe in Life—

Be comfortable—

All is One

## SAME OLD BLUES

I turned on the news
  for the first time in weeks
    and was not surprised to find
      it was still the same old blues

Government in gridlock

The Republicans blaming the Democrats
  The Democrats blaming the Republicans
    and strangely enough
  they're both right—
It's all of them who are to blame
  for not compromising
    and working together daily
      for the good of us all

And we too are to blame
  for we elected them

And—
  as for those of you who didn't vote—
    you are to blame, as well—
      The outcome could have been different

Disasters
  floods
    earthquakes
      famine
    war
  mass shootings—
stock market upturns
  unemployment downturns
    and partly cloudy skies
      with the usual coastal fog—
    no chance of rain tomorrow
  expect the normal seasonal temperatures
and a five-day forecast showing strong signs
  of a predictable continuation—
    of the same old blues

## THE BLACK SHEEP
### (In memory of Douglas M. Schwegel)

Why is poetry the ugly duckling of the Arts?
  Shunned
    Ignored
      Ridiculed
        Laughed at

Why do I see the following words
  at the head of a newspaper column?

  *Editor's note: We do not encourage*
    *contributors to send poems*

Why is poetry
  treated like dirty laundry
    concealed in a hamper
      not to be seen or touched?
    Or like a crazy uncle
  kept in a back room
rarely
  if ever
    seen by the neighbors?

Why is poetry the black sheep
  treated like someone who took a bad turn
    gambles too much
drinks too much
  can't hold a job
    or keep a relationship together?

And why do I bother writing it?

I write it—
  because I've always known—
    that even if you don't need it—

        I do

# TIME IS THE TEACHER

Time is the teacher
(and you its captive audience)

The World is your classroom
(and Life— the major subject)

You are the student
(stay awake and pay attention)

and by the way—

this teacher called Time
couldn't care less
whether you learn
or not

And the bell only rings—

once

# TWO NEW QUESTIONS

For every answer
  there are two new questions

Waves of change
  these questions bring

And there are as many questions
  as there are grains of sand
    in the seven seas
And as many as there are stars
  in the deep skies of night
    and perhaps more so

Questions are the foundation of learning
  Answers are the foundation of knowing

To learn and to know
  is to strive and to live
    to exist
      to be

Choose a star to ponder
  Sift the shifting sands through your fingers

For each question
  may you find understanding

  and for each answer

  may you find

    two new questions

# SELECTED POEMS

# FROM

# Raking Leaves - Poems (2004)

*Each of us inevitable*
*Each of us limitless—*
*Each of us with his or her right*
*upon the earth*
                    -Walt Whitman

## YESTERDAY'S NEWS

In some cultures
   you are born a piece of clay
      and shaped into something useful
A vase
   A water jar
      A decanter

As the years go by
   you may add brushstroke
      after brushstroke
and with creativity and effort
   elevate yourself
      from useful and plain
         to useful and of worth
A work of Art
   A symbol of patience and practice
      A proud part of the culture

Why do we all seem like newspapers?
Picked up
folded and unfolded
Carried under the arm of the work world

Folded and unfolded daily
   Pawed through
      Parts of us torn out
      Ripped from us
   Some pages never seen
Most only glanced at

In a stack
   Available everywhere
      On every corner
   For about the same price
With about the same stories

Day after day
   Year after year
      folded

unfolded
　folded
　　unfolded

Folded one last time and discarded
　or left alone on a park bench
　　to blow away in the wind and rain

Yesterday's news

　I don't want to be—

　　yesterday's news

## INSPIRATION POINT

Yosemite is a dream come true
  A fantasy realized

A paradise lost
  that has been given form
    in a whimsical tale

It is so real that it seems unreal

It seems that—
  every now and then—
    you need to pinch yourself
      to believe that this miracle
        spread out before you
          actually exists

The vastness of this valley
  somehow comes into contact
    with the vastness of your soul

It's more than a place—

      —it's a feeling

And with that feeling filling your soul
  you stand there—
    not knowing what to say

You open your mouth—

    but all that comes forth—

        is a breathless

          wondrous

            sigh

# WANDERING
## (Through the Streets of San Francisco)

Wandering through the streets of San Francisco
with the tight knots of tourists
couples and families
all on their way to a Saturday night dinner
and so am I

The streets down here in Chinatown
have an odd light to them at this time
A different atmosphere
A different feel

When I can separate myself
from the tight knots on the sidewalk
I pick up the pace
throwing my feet out in front of me
as I'm now on the move
for an evening walk through The City

I reach a point where a change begins
Chinatown blending into North Beach
and I walk into City Lights bookstore
making my way back to the poetry section

There, I look through the shelves
to find where my book may sit one day
Hmmmm— right next to Shelley
A nice neighbor to have

Looking through the shelves
I find a book by a San Francisco poet
*Winter Place* by Genny Lim
I buy it and move on
in search of Twice Cooked Pork

I find it on the corner of Broadway and Columbus
A bowl heaped with steaming rice
and a carafe of hot sake
The first sip singes my empty stomach

The cook is singing Chinese opera, I think
and later walks up and asks: *Is food good?*
I look up from the book
and give him the "thumbs-up" sign
　　*It's excellent,* I say with a smile
　　*Thank you*


The fortune cookie lays on a tray with the bill
I crack it open and pull out the paper
whispering between the pieces of cookie
The fortune?
A perfect one
for a bachelor out on the town:
　　*There is a true and sincere friendship*
　　　　*between the two of you*
I set it down on the plate
lift my sake cup
look at my reflection in the window and say
　　*How true—*
　　*Here's lookin' at you, kid!*
I drink a toast to my reflection
and it drinks one to me


Crossing Broadway
a barker at a strip joint beckons me
　　*C'mere, sir— Take a free look*
　　*Take a free look at some nook, sir*
　　*It'll knock ya out!*
I smile and pass him by
and turn up Grant Street
The darker, quieter side
The North Beach Grant Street
The blues clubs
Pizza joints
Coffee houses
Completely different on this side of Broadway


Up the hill I hike to Edith Alley
and knock on the door of Freddie's place
No Answer—
I leave a note and move on

Standing under a streetlight in North Beach
I make a few notes to myself
and walk about
looking up at all the warmly lit houses
Looking up each entry stairway
wondering what the houses are like inside
while knowing that none of them are home to me

I climb—
step after step
and find myself at the base of Coit Tower
Its light illuminating the fog
I look over the blanket of tiny lights
on the rolling hills of The City
all made fuzzy by that fog

And then I climb down the other side
step
   after
      step
         after
            step
               after
                  step

First red brick steps
  then worn wooden ones
    stepping
       down
          down
          down
              into the past
                 and farther down
into the outskirts of the downtown district

I walk past the homeless lost souls
curled up in the openings
of the vaulted lobbies of decadence
unique to the Financial District
and walk on—
picking up my pace

throwing my feet out in front of me
up through Chinatown—
darker— more mysterious now—
It's later

I walk into the Stockton Tunnel
which sounds hollow and cavernous
(even without traffic)
I am the only soul walking in it
and the lights above
blur into a straight line with distance
like passing days—
distinct and separate
clear when near
but blending into onecontinuousblurryline
as Time places distance
between us and them

I reach my truck
with the book tucked under my arm
alone on the ninth floor
of the Sutter-Stockton Garage
and drive down
     down
  down
nine floors

Seven in a continuous left-hand turn
like gliding down the stripes of a candy cane
and I find myself here—
sitting in my rocking chair
with my leg muscles still vibrating
from the steps and steep hills
notebook on my lap

Feeling the experience of life—
taking it all in—
as I write about wandering—
through the streets of San Francisco

## STURDY POEMS

A box arrived today
sturdy— in one piece—
all the way from St. Petersburg, Florida
to California
From the Atlantic to the Pacific
Coast to coast

And in that sturdy box
nestled in soft packing
a sturdy book

And in that sturdy book
spread over soft, yellowing pages
sturdy poems

And although the book is fifty years old
and some poems nearly ninety
the poems remain sturdy—
still traveling through time
still living and breathing
still boasting and bragging
still loving and caressing
weeping, smiling, laughing and touching

On its spine it says:
    Complete Poems - Carl Sandburg

You are a wind gone down; I tell you—
a bucket of ashes—
but your poetry still rises daily—
still illuminates— crimson and orange

And a little bit of you lives on
in the souls of all who read
in the souls of all who breathe
in the souls of all who touch and feel
your sturdy poems

Carl Sandburg— I thank you

## CORPORATE TEAM PLAYERS

Around a long table we professionally sit
    with practiced looks of patience on each face
None of us believing a word of it all
    or wanting to be here in the first place

## TO TRULY CREATE

They can teach you
  Counterpoint and Harmony
    and how the Majors and minors relate
But they cannot teach you how to feel
  and you must feel—
    to truly create

## AND SOME PEOPLE

Some people want to sit back
  and have all handed to them in life
Some people want their bread buttered
  without having to pick up the knife

# THEATRE THOUGHTS

On hot afternoons
  I like to sit in cool theatres
    with Bogart or DeNiro on the screen
To get away from life
  for just a few moments
    and immerse myself in someone else's dream

And forget about those times
  when we acted so familiar
    It's strange how we pretend we're strangers now
We had a blast of passion
  blow up in our smiling faces
    I guess it wouldn't have worked out anyhow

In the quiet of the theatre
  leaving all the noise outside
    I find a chair to settle in and sink
Sometimes I come in here
  just to leave the world outside
    and sometimes I come in here just to think

Sometimes you need a break
  from all the wonder and the worry
    as you wonder what it is life's really worth
If you wander—
  a rolling stone gathers no moss
    If you gather—
      you'll never see this Earth

You try to look to love
  for a solution or an answer
    (Most nights you end up with your loneliness)
Most nights it's just you
  in your world, all alone
    and some nights you settle for something less

Passion plays a foolish song
  in the hearts of many men
    and leaves you memories you'll not soon forget

Yes, it plays a foolish song
  in the hearts of women too
    Nights to remember—
      and dark nights to regret

It all seems so simple
  when your biggest worldly worries
    are pimples, dates, and cramming for exams
When you think you know it all
  when life isn't quite as fragile
    Before life puts you in its little binds and jams

But when the curtain finally falls
  the lights go up and life's not over
    You hit the street and head on home for dinner
Life ain't all that bad
  once you get a little grip
    and realize you are only a beginner

A bird sings out my window
  Curtains rustle in the breeze
    Sunlight changes as it passes through stained glass
Changes suck the sand
  right out from under your feet
    Flow with the river
      for all eras
        shall pass

## BUSTER'S NEWSSTAND

Down at Buster's Newsstand
  the boys got big talk goin' 'round
'bout the Big Rose bitin' the Big One
  yeah— but I bet he'll be back next year
And if not—
  I'll tell ya, there's a guy
    who wouldn't be hurtin' without it
I bet he writes a book about it
  and makes a couple o' million clear

Down at Buster's Newsstand
  talk gets hot and opinionated
and women don't always come in here
  unless they need a cab or a tow
And whenever a babe walks in
  all eyes are up and down her
But the boys don't mean any harm
  they're just lookin', don't ya know?

Down at Buster's Newsstand
  they got politics under control
They know what they mean—
  but if you ask them *Why?*
    they might say— *Just because*
They don't read much beyond headlines
  and usually wake up later
and only now—
  they're seeing The Orange One
    just for what he was

Down at Buster's Newsstand
  sports are what they talk the most
and then cars and women and politics
  but they usually start out with the weather
and then: *Ya hear 'bout Barney passin' on?*
  *Yeah— Where's Joe?*
    *He's on vacation*
  *I hope he and his wife have patched things up*
*I hear they ain't getting' along together*

Down at Buster's Newsstand
  they swap motor mending methods
old war stories
  jokes
    power tools
      and gripe 'bout bein' underpaid
And how if they won the lotto
  they'd take a leak on the Old Man's desk
and head straight away for Tahiti
  *Oh, Man! I'd have it made!*

Down at Buster's Newsstand
  they talk 'bout huntin' and fishin'
Some go for ducks or salmon or bass
  but most of them just go for deer
But truth is, most go to get away
  and only shoot off their mouths
and end up every season
  only baggin' a big case o' beer

Down at Buster's Newsstand
  they complain about their wives
How they do weird things
  or stay quiet for a time
    without ever givin' a reason
How they charge their cards
  up to the limit
    and how they want everything done
around the house, garage and in the yard
  at the height of football season!

Down at Buster's Newsstand
  they talk about their kids
How they hope they do something with their lives
  and stay the Hell away from drugs
But there comes a time
  when a guy walks in
    who had to bail out his kid
and the group all shuffles their feet uneasy
  as he looks down at his
    and shrugs

Down at Buster's Newsstand
   sometimes it gets a little loud
when things get agitated
   and times are gettin' tough
*You see what they want for insurance?*
   *You see what they want for a house?*
*WELL, THEY CAN JUST KISS MY ASS*
   *'CUZ I BEEN KISSIN' THEIRS LONG ENOUGH!!!*

I'm going down to Buster's Newsstand
   for a soda and a candy bar
and if someone comes in or calls for me—
   just tell 'em I'm in the john
And if I don't come back—
   I won the lotto—
      but I might just be hangin' 'round
'cuz down at Buster's Newsstand
   someone always knows
         what's goin' on

## POETRY IS FOR SISSIES

So, poetry is for sissies, you say
  For little old ladies
    over tea and biscuits
    For degree holders
      or eccentrics

Nonsense!

Poetry is within you—
  Each and every one of you

It was in your last breath
  It is in this one
    and it will be in your next one

It is in your blood
  your heart
    your soul

You speak it daily—

  (but are probably unaware of it)

## SAN FRANCISCO MORNING IN L.A.

I had an idea that just drifted away
  on this San Francisco morning
    down in foggy L.A.

So, I shaved and showered
  and hit the streets
    to find a cup o' coffee
      and something to eat
which brought back a memory
  as I remembered soon
    that this part of town
      doesn't open 'til noon

Then I wandered past Wilcox and Hollywood
  and found a place whose coffee
    was reasonably good
with handwritten signs hanging on the wall
  **NO SHOES - NO SERVICE**
    but that's not all...

**SPECIALS - ADD 20 CENTS AFTER ELEVEN**

**NOTHING LARGER THAN A 50**
  **NO 20s AFTER SEVEN**

**2 BACON - 1 EGG  $1.25**

**TOAST, RICE OR POTATOES**
  **ARE ALL ON THE SIDE**

**THOSE BEATING THEIR FOOD BILLS**
  **WILL FACE ARREST**

**COME TASTE THE DIFFERENCE**

**OUR BURGERS ARE THE BEST**

**BEEF BOWL  $2**

**NO BUS CHANGE GIVEN**

**DON'T ASK FOR NOTHIN' FREE**
**WE ALL WORK HERE FOR A LIVIN'**

After two cups of coffee
  I come out of my daze
    as I look at L.A.
      with its hills in a haze

I came down here to visit
  and wander from home
To see friends
  rest my mind
    and write this poem

To just take a break
  hit the road
    and get away
   on this San Francisco morning
down in foggy L.A.

# DEEPER

After flipping a few more burgers
and frying a few more fries
he moves to the back door of the kitchen
wide open
wipes his hands on his greasy apron
and spits into the darkness

Looking up one end of the alley
and then down the other
he walks out and leans against a dumpster
reaching into his shirt pocket
for half a joint

He lights it—
and pulls the smoke deeper—
a siren swells and fades
tires screech
(deeper)
into the night and its drone
(deeper)
a rat scurries across the alley
(deeper)
that's enough—
don't want to lose it in a coughing fit
Ahh—
Yes!
Just a few more hours
a few more burgers
then maybe I can get some—
(Some what?)
some— something
I dunno

Hot summer night
sticky air
no breeze
I gotta get some—
(Some what?)
some— something

Face turning red
eyes watering
can't hold it any longer
but it's only half a joint
gotta make it last
[ex-hhhhhale—]

He picks up an empty bottle
and throws it across the alley
shattering into pieces under a dumpster
the rat scurries
quick
confused

He laughs
and draws another puff of smoke
(deeper)
a phone inside rings
(deeper)
a few more hours
(deeper)
then I'll add my tire screeches
to this midsummer-night-in-the-city song
get some beers
get some people together
get some— something

A middle-aged dishwasher
appears in the doorway
framed by the florescence
his silhouette sharply outlined
wiping his soapy hands on his apron

*What the Hell are ya doin'? You crazy?*

*Doin' what?*

*The glass breaking and laughing to yerself*

*Just a rat*

*Smokin' weed again, huh?*

    *Yep*

(deeper)

The older man had seen it before
wasted away his wild years
on drinking and lying and smoking and doping
and being scraped off the floor
of the downtown drunk tank
after which—
all that was left
was a sink and rubber gloves
seven days a week
washing dishes
pots and pans
pulling the plug—
and watching his life go down the drain

But what hurt him more
was seeing these younger guys
passing through
never staying long—
either screwing up
or never showing up to screw up

And it hurt him to watch these younger guys
wasting away their wild years
tossing them away like a cigarette butt
that quickly
that carelessly

He tried to talk to them
but they'd just look at him and laugh
thinking of him as a stupid old man
a lifetime dishwasher

*Man, smokin' that weed makes ya stupid*

    *Yeah, like I need brains to work here*

*You wanna a job like this the rest of yer life?*

    *Hell, The Man ain't gonna give me nothin' better*

*Yeah, but can't ya see who The Man is?*

    *Give me a break!*

*The Man is you!*

    *Spare me the lecture, will ya?*

*Yer The Man that ain't givin' yerself somethin' better!*

    *The Man ain't gonna let me go any higher than this*
    *but I can get me higher than this*
    *Get lost!*

[a laugh]

The older man shook his head
walking back into the glare of the kitchen
muttering to himself
feeling his own life going down the drain—
seeing the younger ones go up in smoke

Deep in the night

    deep in the shadows

        deep

            deep

                deeper

## WINTER MEADOW

A blank sheet of paper

  virgin
    pristine
      barren...

...barren as a winter meadow
    freshly covered
      with silent snow

I'll walk into this meadow
  leaving tracks for you to follow—
    and for me to find

      my way back home

# Selected Poems

# From

# Whispering Sands
## and Other Poems
## (1989)

*Emerge with the swallow*
*There are other worlds*
*and other peoples*
*Not to conquer*
*but to know*
            -Henry Dierkes

# SHANGHAIED
## (The Curse of a Sailor's Life)

Far out on the deep blue ocean
  where the waves will swell as high
as those snow-peaked mountains that poke
  their heads through clouds in the sky
Far from the smell of baked goods
  and a lonely seagull's cry
Far from the sweet, soft hush
  of a gentle young lover's sigh

A man slowly— painfully awakens—
  and tries to lift his head
though it feels as if it's been weighted
  with a half-ton of molten lead
and he feels the ship's cold fo'c'sle floor
  that served as last night's bed
and the rolling motion of the sea
  that fills his heart with dread

And the rolling motion whispered—
  words not to be denied
Fear, anger, and anguish
  seized and froze him deep inside
as through his foggy thoughts—
  he clearly realized
the year
  was eighteen eighty-eight
    and he had been shanghaied

As much as he tried in the past
  somehow, he could not overcome
his need for smoke filled evenings
  and tall bottles of dark rum
And here again his drunkenness
  caused his life to come undone
by having another endless evening
  of rowdiness and fun

How many bottles were there?
  Two— three— or four?
Enough that he couldn't even recall
  his own Mum's name anymore
And how many years had those bottles
  led him time after time before
to waking up
  half-dead and dazed
    on a ship's cold fo'c'sle floor?

The months dragged by
  as they made their way
    down to the dreaded Cape Horn
feeling ragged, rundown, and worthless—
  wasted, weary, and worn
Overworked and underfed
  His clothes tattered and torn
Wishing with every moment
  that he had never been born

And there below— he was lost in dreams
  of sweet, soft lips, so lush
while above the wide wooden decks were awash
  in snow, sleet, and slush
"ALL HANDS!!!" the first mate bellowed out
  and the crew scrambled forth in a rush
commanded aloft with white-hot words
  that would make an old whore blush

And up into the ice-caked lines
  they obeyed all of his commands
beating their fists against frozen canvas
  to keep feeling in their hands
Some would give their own right arm
  to smell the earthy smell of land
and some will certainly never again
  touch any shore of white sand

Now down below
  in water-soaked clothes
    he watches a candle's wax drip

cocking his head to hear gusts of wind
   hoping another sail doesn't rip
and he swears to himself that he'll take the pittance
   that he'll be paid for this trip
and save for the future, a wife, and a farm
   and never again sail on a ship

But he knows he's only fooling himself
   it will all be gone as before
the moment he catches a whiff of rum
   once he has set foot on shore
And if he's lucky—
   he'll wake in the morn
      lying in the soft arms of a whore
and if not—
   he'll wake up half-dead and dazed
      on a ship's cold fo'c'sle floor

He knows he'll live and die as a sailor
   as he knows he never was graced
with the looks, the money or talent
   to live a high life without haste
And his dreams of slipping his arms around
   a young woman's slender, curved waist
will always be broken by a first mate screaming
   GET UP OR I'LL BEAT YA TO PASTE!!!

Such is the life of a sailor—
   to play but never to win
To knock on opportunity's door
   but never be allowed to walk in
To dream of the future, a wife, and a farm
   while knowing it will be as it's been
living the curse of a sailor's life—
   to be shanghaied—

                    again

                 and again

## SITTING ON THE FRONT PORCH SWING
### (In Memory of Frank and Agnes)

Sitting on the front porch swing
on a warm June afternoon
were a woman and a man
married fifty years
Their Golden Year
Their years were golden
Their hair was silver

She sat close to him
with her head on his shoulder
He gazed out across the river
She, down at her hands and wedding band

With a bit of a smile
at the corners of her mouth
she asked
  "If you were to live life
    over again—
      what would you ask for?"

He paused—
and looked into the sky
Then he said
  "No aches or pains"

"Aches or pains?!"
  she exclaimed with a puzzled face
    "That's not very romantic!"

"You didn't say anything about romance"

"I said..." she said

"You said" he said
  "If I could live..."

"I know what I said" she said

They fell silent—

She rested her head on his shoulder again
The smile returning to the corners of her mouth

She sighed gently and said
  "Fifty years—
    Can you believe it?"

"A couple of silly kids" he said

"We weren't silly!"
  she protested
    "We were in love"

"Yes, indeed"
  he replied
    "A couple of silly kids"

She sat up in the front porch swing
and looked into his eyes
As his looked into hers she asked
  "And what's wrong with love?"

"Oh, love—" he replied
  waving his hand as if shooing a fly
    "Love is a blessing and a curse"

"A curse! —Oh—and how is it a curse?"

Looking into her eyes, he answered—
  "You got me, didn't you?"

Smiling—
she placed her head back on his shoulder
patted his chest
and played with a button on his shirt
and said
  "Oh, you're not a curse
    You're my good boy"

She smiled looking down at her hands
He looked out across the river
making a funny face she couldn't see

"And stop making faces" she said

"Oh, how do you know I'm making faces?"

"I should know you by now, I should hope"

"I suppose you can read my mind, as well"

"Hasn't been anything exciting in there for years"
    she said

She rose and walked across the porch
    He gazed up at her with mock surprise
She smiled and walked in the front doorway
    He smiled and leaned back—
        arms behind his head—
            sitting on the front porch swing

# THE OLD RED BOMBER

I sold the Old Red Bomber today
My first car
That ugly little critter
One hundred seventy-six thousand miles
and a million memories

On my first ride home
I charged up San Francisco hills
and stalled her out
in the middle of an intersection
Felt like a fool
But, hey— I'd never driven a stick before
Give me an "A" for effort, will ya?
I did

I learned about mechanics
from my brothers with her
whether I liked it or not—
I was always short on cash to do otherwise
and who can afford real mechanics
but the rich and the mechanically inept?

I cursed and loved that thing
A true love-hate relationship
that car and I had
She died out on me once
at ten o'clock on a Sunday night
on the Oakland Bay Bridge
I—was—not—happy

She was ugly, faded and worn
Her roof leaked
Rotted the carpet on the passenger's side
Smelled like a swamp on warm rainy days
Luckily, there aren't many warm rainy days
in San Francisco
Rainy days, yes
Warm rainy days?
Not often

And when you don't have a garage
or a driveway
and the weekend is the only free time
you have to work on her
and it's one of those rain-all-weekend
sort of San Francisco weekends
the hate part of the relationship
was in full bloom

How many busted knuckles
from wrenches slipping?
How many aching backs
from leaning into the engine compartment
on a cold, gray, rainy San Francisco Sunday?
How many shivering moments
crawling under her on wet pavement?
Too many
Far too many

But she got me around for six years
and she was ten when I bought her
Seven hundred and fifty dollars
from a fellow named Wendall
She was the ugliest car I ever saw
but she got me around
She and my brother George and I
went clear up to Mount Shasta
Mount Lassen, too
Not to mention Yosemite and Lake Tahoe

Yeah, that old girl got us around
Not without many a mysterious
mechanical moment
I can guarantee you that
Many a mechanical mystery
found by patience or luck
and then— VA-RRROOOOMMMM
she started again
and purred like a kitten
but— Ooooo! Weeee! — was she ugly!

Rusted out roof
Three hubcaps
You had to sort of guess at what color she was
She was sort of red
But she got me around
and she taught me a lot

A high school boy named Bobby came by
and asked what I wanted for her
I said "Three hundred"
He said "I'll take it"
and he liked her so much
that I dropped it down to two-fifty

Four cylinders
Four speed
Four doors
and never to be for-gotten—

The Old Red Bomber

## WHISPERING SANDS

I'm so tired of the aimless way
   life has been treating me
I've been pushed and prodded down a path
   I never thought I'd see
But I haven't stopped doing what I wish
   with the time I have left on my hands
and I'm longing for my feet to walk
   upon the whispering sands

Far from this brittle landscape
   spreading out like a dreaded disease
I want to sit and watch the clouds
   as I embrace a breeze
But here I am in a place so thick
   I can hardly make my way through it
I am just another tooth in the gear
   who is only adding to it

And I wonder what really keeps a person
   bound to such a place
when they could be drawing drafts of air
   pine scented and laced with a trace
of wildflowers and cherry blossoms
   or the saltiness of the seas
allowing their troubles to fall away
   with such unchallenged ease

I long to pull my shirt over my head
   and feel the sun on my skin
instead of being here, chained behind a desk
   and spending my days locked in
an office where I only see the sun
   shining outside of tall, wide windows
I long to be where the hawk flies free
   and where the wild wind blows

Long ago, I took my handsome watch
   and threw it into a drawer
Now all I wish to see rushing

are waves rushing to the shore
I no longer wish to hear sirens howl
    engines moan or tires screech
Give me a silent sunset's glow
    with gulls gliding over the beach

Some people can't leave the city's drone
    but I would not think it strange
for one to wish for the chance to sit
    and watch the seasons change

I've heard the moan
                    and groan
                            and drone
I've obeyed and been bent by demands

Now I only wish—

    to hear the waves

        as I walk—

            upon whispering sands

## DRAGON SMOKE

As a child
I was always curious
about manhole covers
or rather what was beneath them
What lurked under the streets?

You never saw anyone come out of them
or anything, for that matter
Only dragon smoke—
and that was only in the winter
I don't recall any dragons
living under the streets in the summer
I don't know where they went then
Maybe farther north
Maybe Alaska
Maybe the Yukon
Probably not the North Pole
I don't think there are many manhole covers
at the North Pole
and only a few in the Yukon

Dragons like manhole covers
They need someplace to lurk
and with the World being civilized and all—
it's tough for a dragon
to find a large enough cave these days

Dragons don't like being pestered by people
The only dragon I ever heard of
that liked people was Puff
He was a magic dragon in a song
It was popular when I was a kid
and back then—
my dad used to play the song on guitar
and sing it around the campfire during the summer
But that was just a dragon in a song
and he only liked one kid anyway
Nice song, though

We had a manhole cover on Edgar Street
out in front of the house I grew up in
No dragons lived under it
There was never any dragon smoke
Not even in the winter

I used to peek into one of the holes in the cover
while allowing the second hole to let some light in
but that little bit of light didn't do much good—
I wised up and got some matches

I would light a match
drop it in one hole
and peek into the other
Lucky for me there were no gas mains down there
or KA-BLAM!!!
me and that manhole cover
would have gone right through the clouds
on a magic carpet ride to heaven

What did I see?
No dragons
I can tell you that much
It was lined with bricks
and had rusty iron rod steps
going down to the bottom
Not big enough for dragons
I could see that right away
I dropped a few more matches
and looked down there
at the steps
the bricks
the cobwebs
the dust
and the flickering flame in the bottom
No dragons
No KA-BLAM!!!

I soon lost interest in that manhole
and never looked in it again
What was the point in it?

There were no dragons
It wasn't big enough for dragons
even if I could find one
or lure one into the manhole
and what would I use for bait anyway?

It wasn't big enough for a fort either
and if it were big enough for a fort
it had one major drawback:
It was next to the curb
not out in the middle of the street
What if you went down there
and someone parked their car over it?
What would you do
when Mom called out for dinner?

I liked storm drains too
They made nice gurgling sounds when it rained
and you could throw leaves and stuff in the gutter
and watch it disappear into the storm drain
Some fun

I liked to look in them too
but I never saw anything interesting
except once
when I saw a rat run out of one
turn around
and run back in—
Must have taken the wrong exit

That was the closest thing I ever saw
to a dragon coming out of the streets
but I don't think rats can make all that smoke—
Naw, no way
That's dragon smoke
I'm sure of it

Dragons
live under manhole covers
and rats live in storm drains
I hear alligators do too

I guess alligators used to be a craze
I mean live baby ones
(not shoes or handbags)
and when they got a little too big
Moms or Dads used to give them the flush
right down the toilet and into the sewers

Not a very nice thing to do
but I guess some of them lived
Maybe they make the smoke

Naw—
No way—
That's dragon smoke

I'm sure of it

## SMALL CHANGE ON THE DRESSER
(In a Skid Row Flophouse Hotel)

Throwing small change on the dresser
  he looks into the dusty mirror
    and fingers a few of the photos
      tucked into the cracked wooden frame
There's dear ol' Ma, God bless 'er
  I'm glad she doesn't know I'm here
    And this one in the fancy clothes—
      Christ, I can't remember her name

Was it Matilda, Maureen, or Melissa?
  I don't know, it might've been Mandy
    Ah— whoever you were, sweet lass
      I hope you're living good out in the 'burbs
If you were here right now, I'd kiss ya
  and pour you a shot o' brandy
    into my cleanest dirty glass
      as we sat out talkin' on the curb

We could watch the cars go by
  and dogs runnin' into the street
    lookin' lost, scared and confused
      and not sure of which way to go
We could see pigeons scurry and fly
  as they scramble for something to eat
    tossed down by an old man, lookin' amused
      as he shuffles, stiffly and slow

We could go to Barney's Beanery
  Have us a chili and a cold beer
    down on Santa Monica Boulevard
      near the joint with all the pancakes
Yeah, we could take in all the scenery
  The sights to see and sounds to hear
    Pick up a magazine or a postcard
      Anything and everything, whatever it takes

We could walk down dazzlin' Hollywood
  look at the sidewalk with all the stars

and I'll tell ya how I had a chance
to work with DeNiro and Keitel
And with the night feelin' young and good
we could dodge between moving cars
and go to my favorite place to dance
I'll close my eyes and find it by smell

Yes, I'll find it by smell
'cos they make the best meals
you've eaten in all your days
The drinks are cool, the lights are low
and the band plays it sassy and hot
We can play it by ear
and see how it feels
as the evening slowly strays
We can stick around here, or we could go
Time is all we really got

We could go back over to my place—

Suddenly, he looked up into the mirror
and saw the last trace of a smile fade
as his weathered face turned to stone
He turned away to stare into space
let the fantasy disappear
and listened to the torn, yellowed window shade
beat itself in the breeze, all alone

He sat down on the edge of the rickety bed
that was home to last winter's mouse
Beneath, the dust was a blanket of gray
and the old springs creaked and complained
Scenes of horror were haunting his head
A dream job and a little dream house
He said he'd do it all one day
but only memories of wishing remained

In his head, the house was drawn and designed
He walked through each room and hall
He once felt the warmth of a fire he'd make
He once smelled the smells that filled it

Somewhere on the long, hard road he resigned
  bowed his head and gave up on it all
    In his life
      his greatest mistake was to wait
        for somebody else to build it

And there—
  he sits alone in the glare
    of a bar's red neon light
      to live with himself and linger—
        through another long, lonely night
      waiting for the world to turn around
    once more, all the way
  when he'll throw small change
on the dresser again
  at the end
    of another long day

## LIFE

You come in screaming
and go out alone
and in between face—
or fear the unknown


## DREAMS

I find it a righteous
and wonderful thing
to believe in the magic of dreams
To see something as it could be—
not just as it is
or seems


## SOME PEOPLE

Some people think we can live
without governments or elections
when we can't even handle
four-way stop intersections

## AS YOU TURN THE PAGE

Beauty—
  like this before me—
    had to be pulled down
      and pounded and pressed
to become this paper I write upon

And further processed and prepared
  to become this page
    words are printed upon

From the placid beauty of the forest
  to the pleasing, peaceful touch
    whispering between your fingers—

                              as you turn the page

# abstract esoterica

## new experimental poems

*One of the fascinations of language
is the unlimited range of its control...
the abstract and the concrete
the insignificant and the vast
the near and the infinitely remote.*
                              -Bonaro Wilkinson

NOTE: Poems in this section titled *Abstract Esoterica* are of an abstract, experimental nature. An experiment in writing *outside* of your thoughts and emotions, rather than writing from *within*, so to speak. *Abstract Commentaries*, if you wish. If any of the poems in this section, in part, or in their entirety, make any sense whatsoever, it is purely an invention of your own imagination— or maybe not.

–JS

## DIAGNOSTIC TWANG

Contrary to self-serving protestations
by lovers of penalized realization—
situational morality *does* exist—
with indulgent
and obvious emotional debates
that may only suggest disingenuous kibitzing—
ultimately damaging any sense
of social celibacy and repressive freedom—
which may curtail a warm and fuzzy prosecution
of intimate connotations—
synonymous with a bubbling transgressive desire
to bemoan legitimate jubilation—
in exchange for grayer clarity—
and surrealistic hype

Meanwhile—
forgetting whispers of intense fear
sandwiched between values and priorities—
an intelligent delicately celebrated
but unlikely recovery
pushed by romantic and crucial acts
of vanishing memories—
grandly changed from eloquence
to a more relaxed harmony—
typical of most incredibly accurate
but condemned requests
to gobble up anything described as hushed—
soulful—
round—
or especially greasy

However—
a dark and dense atmosphere
of collaborative sensibilities—
actually provided
yet another lavish series
of delightful and ridiculously towering—
but ruthless daydreams of dangerous indiscretions
that returned suddenly to a disturbing persona—

that oozes with mainstream all-encompassing
but unnecessary—
easy listening arrangements

Nonetheless—
with tumbling tears of lemonade
and equally besotted lilting lyrics
of pithy equanimity—
engaging in a profound sense
of compressing everything
into anything plagued by
an appropriate pastoral promise
to divulge unexploded alternatives—
and savor a traditional—
but slightly raspy—

diagnostic twang

# IN PERPETUITY

A bid to outlaw spanking stirs concerns
and a deluge of terminal emotions—
declining—
no longer valiant—
but welcome in this crucially parched battle
of senseless consequences
and wide-ranging contradictions—
and that's because significant content was scant
compared with the analysis
threatened by irate neighbors—
who expected a ruling
to adequately impact the likelihood
of sufficiently strong kindness
including no easy struggle—
to be worse than normal

Meanwhile—
another viewing of the targeted generosity—
revealed the crumbling plans
to halt three Johnny-jump-ups
opposed to fierce cursing—
while calling supporters
undisclosed but detailed descriptions—
after a casual obstruction of intention
needed a swirling proliferation of incorrect venting
upon violated works of disputed conversations—
benefiting from the terror and tension
of global confusion over long-haul requirements
and the destruction—
of authentic stagnation

Moreover—
widespread experts
retrieved shared increases in particular resources
to add support automatically accessed
to sample even better harassing
in all kinds of
"Away-you-go" situations—

Ah-Ha! —
and now for a disclaimer—
Not all simulated editorial errors
or performance warranties
are designed to improve destinations—
and will not necessarily operate
applicable statements of corporate behavior
enabled with these restrictions herein—
while approval may vary
*without* due notice of fair transactions
construed as available services—
according to greater than exact representations
based on other practices
reserved for accurately standard satisfaction—
and extending the boundaries
between greenish-orange polarity—
and pungent pervasiveness

Therefore——
without prodding for a starting point
of remaining action in topological spaces—
the emphasis to furnish new material
turned upstream to a position
of central contact—
while applying a theory to stipple together
functioning potentialities—
and mechanical plasticity

Nonetheless—
habitual movements
adapted to change the volume
within appropriate air-filled cavities—
abruptly condensed the vapors
of concentrated awareness
with a systematic uncertainty
of cultural evisceration—
with impunity—

in perpetuity

## IRRESISTIBLE THUMBS

Totally enthusiastic
but overwhelmingly cautious
with an intentional unwillingness—
and with an emphasis
on plenty of shared blame
(and evermore accurate atrocities of competence) —
a handful of tarnished armchair team members
(identifiable but unnecessarily ignored) —
published uninformed and incendiary investigations
into inaccurate reports
of publicly agreed assessments—
(Weeding out inept cheerleaders
and real cowboy rhetoric)—
while it allowed a stabilization
of reality-based arrogance
and the reconstruction of rude—
but optimistic forecasts

Meanwhile—
a suspended approach to the classic
and unapproachable negotiations
for the proposed peaceful prospect—
of protecting perceived and pressing
provocative programs—
continued along an avenue of flexible and quaint
but uncompromising dialogue—
which could either be unable or unwelcome
in a dismissed offer to understand
gestures of intended soft—
but formidable dispute—

However—
avoiding the pretensions
of a currently interested homeowners' market—
already attracted and banging
on unobstructed exits of alternative
but temporary services—
inspected daily to maintain escape
to adjacent areas of tight

but impaired awareness
of the lowest feasible levels—
with special attention to compensate
for additional compartmentalization—
of skittish disappointment

Moreover—
*don't worry*—
just look beyond the finalized slick details
that are insensitive
but supportive of the energy and desire
that habit-forming habits lack—
while representative of properly hung corrosion
concealed leakage
and the scheduled misalignment
of charming dreams—
which include neutral carpeting—
and separate—
retractable—
but distinct accordions

Nevertheless—
purchasing time during these two entire days
might damage untitled niacin chronicles
and really add credence to walnuts—
garlic—
exercise—
and inadvertently release malfunctions
with typically strong achievement
and a discussion
*very different* from widely considered—
and seemingly tremendous—

irresistible thumbs

## HEARTWARMING BELLY WIGGLES

Without expressly authorizing
the undesirable quagmire—
voters recently dominated
an appealing phrasing that distances minds
from the unwittingly successful attack—
on central up-to-the-minute information
mired in an undercurrent of dysfunction—
but still *way* better
than the traditional poverty of truth
subscribed to by thickening molasses—
while trolling for effective ways
to ignore the unease
of hard-working Americans
who are clearly the majority—
but—
who really wants to know?

Meanwhile—
in a subtle but insignificant shift—
personalized irretrievable revelations
foraging for an opportunity
and likely to compete—
with infrequently overwhelmed messages
from a barrage of unfolding contenders
who are vying for a particular—
(and possibly profound) —
unprecedented prosperity
professionally promoted
with unpredictable prospects and proposals—
that thrive in a wave of struggling ideas
but are essentially shipwrecked on the shores—
of generic misperception

However—
let's focus on the broader needs—
serious—
too important to come as no surprise—
but rightly sidetracked
by limiting inadequate attention

under the guise of high-quality
applications of demonstrated failure—
which simply exercises caution
while ignoring the strategy
to curtail regulatory inequalities
among professors of commonly formidable networks—
and those unlucky—
but respectable—
discount housepainters

Moreover—
(and for the time being) —
let's also pay attention to the demand
that defines the common mistake
to identify the accessible and acceptable ways
to think about the astounding development—
of graphically suspended
and recklessly encouraged time investors
who are raising resistance
and refusing to promote profusions of pink—
as well as full-time compensated grandstanding
concerning common bricks of vulnerability—
and terminally hypocritical kisses

Nevertheless—
as a way to return to the original incident
repeatedly approached
but currently challenged
with gestures of resonated hardships—
and other accidentally discovered
impressively constructed
clear-eyed self-insulated structures
of favorably squalid scandals—
methodically purported to be no match
for an avalanche of illegal—
expanding—
but reliably simply filthy secrets—

of heartwarming belly wiggles

## DANGEROUS COBBLESTONES

Engineering an apparently tricky bet
on an emerging rebirth of fiction—
calls for a telling improvisational sensitivity
to steer clear of fluctuating forces—
with a makeshift apocalyptic anonymity
to avoid having to pony up
promised constructed conditions—
beginning with painful reminders
of financial violence—
and intricately detailed renderings
of make-believe worlds
with menacing—
though cheerful family scenes

Meanwhile—
with blazing simplicity
and long-forgotten uncovered poignancy—
a massacre of normality
offers mostly sunny portraits of cluttered conflict
and warnings of molested justice—
carefully assembled as a result
of earlier diggings and prodding
by a dogged advocate of scandalous muffins—
and pleasant memories
of renewed juvenile struggling
with a periodic isolation of sympathetic comfort—
and a withholding of inevitable guessing
within a favorable framework—
of colorful surprises

However—
an equal fondness for elegant proportions
unscrupulous privatization
and fuzzy octagons—
produced profound consequences
of strongly stinking decisions
sumptuously dominated by uncharacteristically
blunt rumors—
but pointing forward

with snappy—
perfectly symmetrical nutty concoctions
of intriguing images
that accurately suffered muted pastel calculations—
alongside a darkish blur of speculated results
with completely invigorating
and well-chosen—
underachieving contempt

Therefore—
let us not forget
that the issue depends on the exaggeration
of centrally acknowledged assumptions—
to change the extreme best guesses of expertise
to intentionally humorous distortions
of semi-circular agendas—
with simply dazzling blank happenings
and far-reaching revelations
including somewhat embellished bravado—
that supports horrifying demonstrations
of proprietary procedures
without grainy ointments—
and less optimistic eagerness
for frenzied chatter—
and rigorously righteous regalia

Nevertheless—
the understandably interchangeable dilemmas
depend on a properly performed policy
of processed responses—
that may lead to an oversimplification
of frivolously superficial calculations
and murky old habits of unabated fervor—
with plenty of precocious and precious missteps
and cleverly increasing but uncompromising integrity
misinterpreted as fascinatingly needless—
with botched and compounded derelict merging
and two different charming views—

of dangerous cobblestones

## SPINNING COMPLEXITIES

Well, how about that?
Another meticulous mainstream process
that hints at a rectangular
but innovative variation of pausing and pondering—
while directly beneath—
layers of incorrect insensitivities and insults
compound the considerations of comfort
bringing the potential to a confusing crawl—
while whistling at malfunctioning imperatives
that rarely feature tranquil
or normally flawed applications—
but hopefully maintain a swinging pendulum
and the *swoosh* of an unnecessarily silent mechanism—
of mediocre responses

Meanwhile—
unusually polite flogging was closely monitored
with nasty threats to impair and affect
the general confident quality—
taken as violations
of subsequently decomposing details
which specifically recognized—
and incorporated—
the dumping of inhumane inquiries
into the commonplace practice
of digging into several jettisoned—
itsy-bitsy reauthorizations
of somewhat exaggerated misfortune—
and exceedingly restrictive impatience

However—
widely acclaimed and freshly muffled
by several decades of certified challenges—
and supported by inappropriate applications
of general preventative maintenance—
all locations launched into a quest
to find and feature an oddity of relative triumph
and novice attempts to create and enhance
a crowd-pleasing dream—

and realize that trusted traditions
of savory responses and bemused urgency
may be gloriously less-than-thrilling—
but probably saturated with unfamiliar quirkiness
and complicated—
but kooky delights

Moreover—
variations of long-term miscalculations
caused by a confirmed number of naughty and neurotic
secondary outsiders—
were declared dynamically well-meaning—
while attempting a catastrophic crossing point
considered treacherous and entangled
compared to a stampede of not-too-magnificent
deputized litterbugs—
who released a mass of inconsistent logs
while increasing spiral activity
with an unclear appreciation
of smoking mechanical pressure—
and circulating domestic exchange

Nevertheless—
cleverly increasing
richly complicated connections
contradicted brutal embellishments—
while questions answer themselves
in delicate depths of distraught and divided despair
disturbingly dependent on delightfully derelict discourse—
and offering eager concentrations of sincerity
but apparently remaining aloof—
while abandoning those shifting and shadowy

spinning complexities

## ILLEGAL RECEPTACLES

An effort underway
is meant to rescue competitive anxiety—
and legally process the impossibly expanding regulations
rotting behind the scenes—
while redefining unharvested scrutinizing
fraught with undocumented reality
and quietly lengthening
the discreetly pursued oversimplification—
of unwieldy tomatoes

Meanwhile—
all sides attempt to factor in
an urgently reduced threatening input—
while stepped-up enforcement
of fractured but minor modernized necessity—
allows for commercializing the industrialization
of centuries of mixed impoverished messages
and an unlikely—
but uniquely positioned truce
between a poignant collection of little words—
and cures for insurmountable
and wildly romantic dreams—
of circumnavigation

And— (by the way)—
everything that shifts across these barriers
separately sounded acceptable
(although icy and aggressively far-fetched)—
and described the odyssey
to rejuvenate reliable environmental issues—
but various parts provided automatic solutions
when participating in individual displays
of seriously distinguished intention—
while outrageously concerned
with the potential danger
of the damages done to hopeful—
yet standard—
windows of memory loss

However—
Problems have revealed violations to reinstate
the refused explanations
of terminated participants—
(many of whom list *disposable gain* as a complaint)
as they stand alone in a timely failure
to notify the expressed agency of imminent delay—
while misrepresenting improperly focused
and eventually promised practices—
with adequately incorrect abuses
of private grievances and canceled cases
of denied answers with average—
but suspended disorder

Nevertheless—
an optional offering to *chit-chat*
while cooperating with unlimited
and deeply contested validity—
was beleaguered with renewed innovations
of unopposed corruption
as challenges to negotiate bohemian insolence
were suddenly criticized as significant—
(although pretty meaningless)
galvanizing and progressive
(but mistakenly bankrupt of critical decisions)
a gathering force of key sensibilities
(with reasonable but relentless impact)
and fearful of cosmic explanations
particularly frightening
in the aftermath of a voluminous immersion
into the echoing parables

of illegal receptacles

# MUDDY ACHIEVEMENT

Let's get a glimpse of promised enticements
while basking in the misled glow
of profusely defrauded renovation—
linked to an extravaganza of intimidation
amid concerns that highlight everything
from smoothly important strategies—
to a seemingly misguided empowerment
boosted by charismatic
and controversial characteristics—
with a number of grievances
assumed to be prominent
and clothed in an infusing darkness
of youthful discipline—
relatively extended by simultaneous
and immense open flame sculptures
of magical transformation—
and exuberant sleepless nights

Meanwhile—
An extreme revamping
of monotonous memorized slog—
proudly acknowledged as necessary
and suspended in screaming new ideas
that were overwhelming but dismissed
as potentially legitimate—
and eligible to be quoted for odious spouting
of a variety of misperceptions—
if shaken and shown to be stylized and infected
by cheekily intimate risqué intensity—
which unfolds to complicate the simplest rhetoric
of the most captivating and perpetual—
understated frenzy

However—
an exceptional legacy of painful dreaming
could lead to effortlessly rhyming such words as:
       tune/soon
       destroyed/employed
and   firm/squirm

while threatening heavy and sustained
performances of historic decompression—
inside a relatively low
but brilliantly ancestral valley of soaring reductions—
while overlooking the preserved experience
of significant and unique integrity—
unable to guarantee the tentative and silent coalition
involved in changing chances to undo
the perfectly backward guesses—
despite comfortable wishes
lambasted by decades of distrust
and the original echoes of undeveloped
but not-so-terribly juicy—
back-alley circumstances

Therefore—
simply pointing the finger
ignores the passing radical request
and candid questioning
thought to be a vertical defensive gain—
(cagey and rather uninspired)
but assumed to be joyous
with fist-pumping delirium
and frustratingly healthy razzing—
instantly calculated as ineffective displeasure
with a diagnosis to turn around and say
          *Bullocks!*
with a minimum of concern—
for comforting noise

But let us not forget—
that fragile attention providing as-yet-unbuilt
crashing waves of earmarked focus—
has gotten nowhere—
with plenty of privately managed backflush
and perpetually expansive prestigious prowess—
conveniently scratching
dozens of slick-backed and dilapidated denizens
of an abandoned quirky history—
who wouldn't know a box of chocolate macaroni—
from an Italian marble ceiling

Nevertheless—
this only underscores a miscellaneous discussion
of an incredibly inundated inspirational individual—
who somehow hopes to eagerly explore
the flummoxed organization
of traditional shortcomings—
with compounded and botched
but sublime astonishment—
and take a commanding and cautionary vision
of contrasting disadvantaged psychological overtones—
and sweeping through a rudimentary maze
to satisfy the restructuring of no-holds-barred
do-it-yourself grassroots handholding—
lightly revised but similarly upgraded
with jerky and increasingly integrated
cursed predictability—
with a demure configuration of tailored interests
frequently full-blown motivations—
enormous popping noises—
and unprecedented, majestic transactions

of muddy achievement

## COLOPHON

The
font used
for the text is
**Georgia**, created in
1993 by Matthew Carter
The font used as display type is
## Baveuse
created in 2003 by Ray Larabie
Cover design by Aberration Studio
www.aberration.studio
Cover photo © Janet McCall
Designed in Spring 2024

**www.jackshiner.com**

## ABOUT THE AUTHOR

Jack Shiner (pronounced: Shī-ner) is a retired Stationary Engineer born in Royal Oak, Michigan. He was raised there and in Leelanau County, Michigan. He currently lives in northern California with his wife Jan. He is a poet and song-writer. This is his fourth book of poetry to be published.

www.ingramcontent.com/pod-product-compliance
Lightning Source LLC
Chambersburg PA
CBHW021502090426
42739CB00007B/428